OPENING CRE

Contributors this issue: Simon J. Ballard, Rachel Bellwoar, David Michael Brown, James Cadman, Dawn Dabell, Jonathon Dabell, David Flack, John H. Foote, John Harrison, Julian Hobbs, Kev Hurst, Darren Linder, Brian J. Robb, Allen Rubinstein, Peter Sawford, Aaron Stielstra, Ian Taylor, Dr Andrew C. Webber. Caricature artwork by Aaron Stielstra.

All articles, photographs and specially produced artwork remain copyright their respective author/photographer/artist. Opinions expressed herein are those of the individual.

Design and Layout: Dawn Dabell
Copy Editor: Jonathon Dabell

Most images in this magazine come from the private collection of Dawn and Jonathon Dabell, or the writer of the corresponding article. Those which do not are made available in an effort to advance understanding of cultural issues pertaining to academic research. We believe this constitutes 'fair use' of any such copyrighted material as provided for in Section 107 of the US Copyright Law. In accordance with Title U.S.C Section 107, this magazine is sold to those who have expressed a prior interest in receiving the included information for research, academic and educational purposes.

Printed globally by Amazon KDP

A Word from the Editing Room

Welcome to Issue 4 of Cinema of the '70s. If this is the first issue you've bought, we're glad to have you aboard and hope you'll like what you see enough to become part of our ever-expanding readership. If you've been with us a little longer, thanks for coming back and continuing to support our independent print publication. It means so much to have so many enthusiastic, valued readers around the globe.

In our latest edition, we're delighted to introduce three writers who are new to the mag. Kev Hurst gives his thoughts on David Cronenberg's potent bloodcurdler *The Brood* (1979), Peter Sawford examines the sublime two-handed thriller *Sleuth* (1972) and Andrew C. Webber marks his debut with a look at Robert Altman's *California Split* (1974). Three cracking articles, we're sure you'll agree! Other goodies served for your reading pleasure include articles on the Carry On movies from the decade, the *Planet of the Apes* sequels, *The Hunting Party* (1971), *The Deep* (1977), *Hooper* (1978), *Joe Kidd* (1972) and many more!

It is almost one year to the day since the first issue was released. Time really does fly! With over half a century elapsing since the '70s began, it was always at the back of our mind that there might not be many people left who'd care enough, or have enough interest, in reading about and revisiting movies from that era. But the exact opposite has turned out to be true - '70s cinema enthusiasts are alive and kicking, and we're ecstatic to know there are so many of them out there. What could be better, more heartening, than continuing to discover fans of this incredible era of cinema, people who love the creativity, grit, craft and power of '70s films?

Anyway, without further ado it's time to leap into another packed edition of '70s goodness. Enjoy!

Dawn and Jonathon Dabell

Remembering Jean-Paul Belmondo (1933-2021)

On 6th September, 2021, Jean-Paul Belmondo died at the age of 88. Considered an icon and a national treasure in his native France, Belmondo stubbornly resisted the lure of Hollywood despite being coveted for decades by the biggest studios in Tinseltown, instead concentrating on a mainly Euro-centric career. He got his breakthrough in the French New Wave classic *À bout de souffle* aka *Breathless* (1960) and remained very active throughout the '60s, '70s, '80s and '90s. He suffered a stroke in 2001 but, despite difficulty walking and speaking, continued acting until his final feature in 2009 (*Un homme et son chien/A Man and His Dog*). He was a multiple award winner and nominee, picking up a César, honorary Palme d'Or and Golden Lion accolades, and two BAFTA nominations. His '70s films were:

Borsalino (1970)
Les mariés de l'an deux/The Scoundrel (1971)
Le casse/The Burglars (1971)
Docteur Popaul/Scoundrel in White (1972)
La scoumoune/Hit Man (1972)
L'héritier/The Inheritor (1973)
Le magnifique/The Man from Acapulco (1973)
Stavisky (1974)
Peur sur la ville/The Night Caller (1975)
L'incorrigible/Incorrigible (1975)
L'alpagueur/The Hunter Will Get You (1976)
Le corps de mon ennemi/Body of My Enemy (1976)
L'animal/Animal (1977)
Flic ou voyou/Cop or Hood (1979)

RIP Monsieur Belmondo. Thanks for the memories.

In Memoriam

**Ed Asner
(1929-2021)**
Actor, known for *Skin Game* (1971) and *Gus* (1976).

**Leslie Bricusse
(1931-2021)**
Composer and lyricist, known for *Scrooge* (1970) and *Willy Wonka & the Chocolate Factory* (1971).

**Sonny Chiba
(1939-2021)**
Actor, known for *The Street Fighter* (1974) and *The Bullet Train* (1975).

**Michael Constantine
(1927-2021)**
Actor, known for *Peeper* (1975) and *North Avenue Irregulars* (1979).

**Alex Cord
(1933-2021)**
Actor, known for *The Last Grenade* (1970) and *Chosen Survivors* (1974).

**Richard Donner
(1930-2021)**
Director, known for *The Omen* (1976) and *Superman* (1978).

**Melvin van Peebles
(1932-2021)**
Director and actor, known for *Watermelon Man* (1970) and *Sweet Sweetback's Baadasssss Song* (1971).

**Charlie Robinson
(1945-2021)**
Actor, known for *Sugar Hill* (1974) and *The Black Gestapo* (1975).

**William Smith
(1933-2021)**
Actor, known for *Invasion of the Bee Girls* (1973) and *The Ultimate Warrior* (1975).

**Mikis Theodorakis
(1925-2021)**
Composer, known for *The Trojan Women* (1971) and *Serpico* (1973).

THE HUNTING PARTY

THE BLOOD SQUIBS OF OLIVER REED

by Darren Linder

The Hunting Party, one of my favorite westerns, was overlooked and misunderstood upon its release. The film was reviled and savaged in reviews, and only over time has it been re-appreciated as one of the grittiest westerns with a great ensemble cast. Released in 1971 and directed by Don Medford, this film epitomizes the stark, bloody and unique storytelling style of the early '70s. That year in particular is infamous for films that broke new ground, challenged the viewer's expectations, dealt with uncomfortable or taboo topics and shocked audiences with depictions of graphic violence and sexuality. A short list of game-changers from 1971 would include *Straw Dogs*, *A Clockwork Orange*, *Dirty Harry*, *Harold and Maude*, *The French Connection* and *Walkabout*. The Hunting Party sits comfortably among these.

The three lead actors are Oliver Reed, Gene Hackman and Candice Bergen. Reed was a known force from his recent role in *Oliver!* (1968). He'd also just appeared in Ken Russell's *The Devils*, which is still controversial and unrestored to this day, fifty years later. Hackman had previously starred in *Bonnie and Clyde* (1967), and followed his role in *The Hunting Party* by playing Popeye Doyle in William Friedkin's *The French Connection*. His career was about to skyrocket. Bergen had recently completed the controversial films *Soldier Blue* (1970) and *Carnal Knowledge* (1971). She later played a similar kidnapped character in John Milius' *The Wind and the Lion* (1975). *Murphy Brown* was still a very long way off for her.

The supporting cast is all familiar actors that you've seen before. They include Simon Oakland, L.Q. Jones, Mitchell Ryan, G.D. Spradlin, William Watson and Rayford Barnes. Some of them were the stock faces of films from Sam Peckinpah, Sergio Leone and Francis Ford Coppola.

Oliver Reed is truly one of my favorite actors, and what a workhorse he was. This barrel-chested beast of a man released nearly thirty films in the '70s. That's virtually three films a year on average, some years even putting out

four! Most actors don't get to make thirty films in their entire career, yet Olly did it in one decade. Due to his omnipresence, Reed essentially owns '70s cinema for me. I jotted down some famous actors and the number of films they released during that decade for reference - Al Pacino (8), Paul Newman (10), Dustin Hoffman (11), Robert Redford (12), Clint Eastwood (15), and Jack Nicholson (16). Hackman came close to Reed's record, making 19 films in the '70s. Some of my favorite Reed performances from this period are *The Devils*, *The Hunting Party*, *Sitting Target*, *Revolver*, *Burnt Offerings* and *The Brood*. I would love to curate an Oliver Reed film festival someday, of course finishing up with his amazing performance as Proximo in Ridley Scott's *Gladiator* (2000).

But back to *The Hunting Party*. The set up is simple. Reed's character runs a gang of outlaws who kidnap a schoolteacher played by Bergen. He does this because he wants to learn how to read. Unknown to him, the woman is married to a very wealthy, mean son of a bitch played by Hackman. His character is so rich and powerful that the train, the town and even the county itself is named after him: Ruger. Which is, of course, a famous firearms manufacturer. When Ruger learns that his wife was kidnapped, he gets some hunting buddies together and forms a posse to go after her. He treats it like a hunting expedition, even gifting the fellas with special long-distance hunting rifles fitted with scopes. Ruger doesn't seem like a valiant man trying to save his wife. He seems like a man offended that someone dared to steal his property, and he wants to get it back before its value is depreciated. He worries about her being raped and befouled by these men, even speaking of having to then raise her bastard child. He wants the excuse to hunt men on a safari. He wants to hunt the most dangerous game from a distance like a sniper, picking off the members of Reed's gang anonymously.

Hackman clearly had a blast digging into this unlikable

character. He perfectly embodies an angry, dysfunctional man who is in love with himself. He is a megalomaniac and a narcissist, a capitalist and a misogynistic bastard. But what a meaty role for him to play! Hackman's character in the 1992 film *Unforgiven* feels like a slightly less volatile version of this character, slightly tempered by two decades of aging. Hackman won the best supporting actor Academy Award for that role. I believe that had *The Hunting Party* not been so shunned by the press and dismissed as schlock exploitation, he would have been potentially nominated for this role also.

Watching Reed inhabit his role is mesmerizing. He just looks like a badass riding around on his horse, stern-faced, leading his pack of tired and dirty men. He spends most of his time keeping them in check, breaking up fights, preventing rapes and maintaining control. Once scene has always stayed with me. He is calmly talking to a small subgroup of his men who are about to mutiny. He walks over slowly while talking, holding a plateful of food and a knife. Then, in one fluid motion, he drops the plate, grabs the shotgun from the man with one hand and punches him in the face with the other. I watched that scene repeatedly just to appreciate it fully. I wonder how many takes it took to get the final scene.

When Hackman's character and his posse get within range of Reed's party, they line them up in their scopes and begin assassinating them. We view those characters through the riflescope's crosshairs, making us complicit. We are the shooters. By 1971 America had seen numerous assassinations of political figures, including JFK, RFK, MLK and Malcolm X. One of the first characters to be killed in this movie suffers a headshot which reminded me precisely of the headshot to John F. Kennedy in the motorcade. Whether intentional or accidental, the reference is unmistakable and part of our

country's shared cultural memory.

America had also been seeing the atrocities of the Vietnam War on television news broadcasts, and there was much opposition to our involvement there. During a Vietnam War protest at Kent State in 1970, several college students were shot and killed by the National Guard. Every film must be seen in the context of the time it was released. Western films about outlaw Americans meddling in Mexico could indeed be interpreted as an allegory for American forces meddling in Vietnam. Sam Peckinpah's ultimate classic from 1969 *The Wild Bunch* comes to mind.

The Hunting Party is a direct response to the violence shown in *The Wild Bunch* as well as the violence of the Vietnam War. The Peckinpah influence is vivid and clear. The use of slow motion, quick-cut editing, multi-camera coverage and realistic blood squibs feels like Don Medford was recreating the carnage in the shootouts that bookend *The Wild Bunch*. Specifically, the watering hole massacre in *The Hunting Party* is homage to both the bank robbery shootout and the climactic Battle of Bloody Porch in *The Wild Bunch*. Peckinpah was actually trying to make the violence as graphic and realistic as he could to show people how horrible and devastating real violence is. He refused to romanticize it at all. Interestingly, people embraced it and got off on it rather than shying away from it. Films that came after it had to compete with its level of visual violence, or else be seen as unrealistic or sanitized.

Blood squibs are basically condoms filled with fake blood and a small explosive charge that is detonated remotely or by wires. They are applied to a metallic shield taped to the actor to protect their skin. When detonated it tears through the clothing and squirts out the fake blood, making for far more realistic bullet wounds than any CGI effect

Melissa Ruger (CANDICE BERGEN) kneels over one of the outlaws just killed by her husband in "The Hunting Party"

OLIVER REED · CANDICE BERGEN · GENE HACKMAN · THE HUNTING PARTY

Frank Calder's men push the wagon carrying Melissa Ruger (CANDICE BERGEN) out of the river on to dry land in "The Hunting Party"

OLIVER REED · CANDICE BERGEN · GENE HACKMAN · THE HUNTING PARTY

With his old friend Matthew Gunn (SIMON OAKLAND) looking on, Brandt Ruger (GENE HACKMAN) takes aim and kills one of the men he has hunted down in "The Hunting Party"

OLIVER REED · CANDICE BERGEN · GENE HACKMAN · THE HUNTING PARTY

Frank Calder (OLIVER REED) gingerly probes the side of Doc (MITCHELL RYAN) for an elusive and fatally mortal bullet in "The Hunting Party"

OLIVER REED · CANDICE BERGEN · GENE HACKMAN · THE HUNTING PARTY

Doc (MITCHELL RYAN), with the aid of a persuasive shotgun, helps to unclench with some gang trouble in "The Hunting Party"

OLIVER REED · CANDICE BERGEN · GENE HACKMAN · THE HUNTING PARTY

In a genius move, Medford has several scenes where characters are just speaking dialogue and we don't know that the hidden snipers are ready to attack. So right in the middle of a line reading someone's head explodes with a blood squib hidden in his hair. Or a shirtless character in the background had a blood squib attached to his stomach, camouflaged by makeup so that it blends with his skin. Directors always hide the squib charge under the person's clothing, so seeing it go off directly on someone's bare skin is shocking. After a few of these scenes, you are drawn in and the tension is ratcheted up as you expect a blood squib to explode at any moment. It's just a waiting game until the next bullet wound. No character is immune to it.

Another similarity this film shares with *The Wild Bunch* is its unflinching view of the violence itself. Not only are the blood squibs some of the best I've seen, but the wound makeup is believable and realistic. None of that bright red fake blood that some '70s films are famous for. Both films show the graphic and brutal side of what gunfights actually cause. These films strike at the more palatable John Wayne westerns where people would get shot bloodlessly, grab their chest, then fall over and die instantly. In these films, there is indeed blood, both at the point of entry and the exit wound. And people do not die instantly. They suffer and bleed out slowly, needing to be dragged by their comrades, thus slowing down the group. Sometimes untrained medical care is attempted, the wound gets infected, or a friend will ask to be mercy

killed. Medford's camera even focuses on strange little unglamorous moments like a man's leg twitching as he dies, or a man scrabbling on the dirt dying with a large desert insect crawling across his chest. The viewer, like the characters, watches these men's death throes like a scientist watching a test subject. One even says: "It's not like killing an animal, is it?"

Watching this film in the context of the Vietnam War noticed another interesting connection. The use of long-distance weapons to pick off the enemy parallels certain things done for the first time during the Vietnam War Specifically, the use of helicopters and napalm. To quote *Apocalypse Now*, the US Cavalry "traded in their horses for helicopters and went tear-assing around 'Nam looking for the shit." There was the relative safety, or at least distancing, of flying around in helicopters firing down upon enemy soldiers with machine guns and missiles. Foot soldiers on the ground could do little to retaliate against the steel death from above. The use of napalm was even more devastating and impossible to defend against. Air Force jets would drop napalm canisters on the jungle and be a mile away before the explosions were finished. So in *The Hunting Party*, these super-rifles with telescopes on them could represent the US military's use of long distance technology to attack targets without fear of reprisal. For the gun enthusiasts, the sniper weapon in the film is the Sharps-Borchardt .54 caliber rifle, supposedly accurate up to 800 yards,

Even though I knew this movie was a British-American production, it struck me as having a spaghetti flavor. Later, when I became a devotee of those bloody Italian westerns, I realized the two reasons for this. First, the soundtrack is by Riz Ortolani, often considered the #2 Italian composer

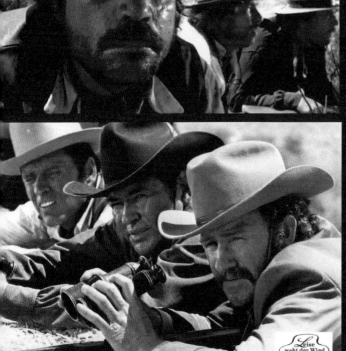

after Morricone. Ortolani scored 237 movies, while Morricone scored over 500. The second reason is that it was filmed in Almeria, Spain. Any spaghetti western worth its gunpowder was filmed in this region. I recognized the white stone buildings from the Leone Dollars Trilogy, and half expected Lee Van Cleef to come riding around the corner in a cameo. Reed even resembles Gian Maria Volonté from the first two films of the Dollars trilogy. So you could class this film as an honorary spaghetti western and get away with it.

One obvious downside is the treatment of women. There is a lot of slapping, terrorizing, gratuitous nudity, threat of rape, two actual rape scenes and the Stockholm syndrome with the Bergen character eventually falling for Reed. It certainly isn't a perfect film but has enough great qualities to deserve to be re-appreciated and enjoyed by fans of the genre.

The Hunting Party is full of unique cinematic moments. A woman in a blood-covered white dress holding a knife just after killing a man brings to mind Brian De Palma's movie *Carrie*. Hackman's character actually gets Reed in his sights several times but hesitates and doesn't fire. He wants to prolong the game and have a face-to-face confrontation, so that his quarry knows exactly who is about to kill him. A dead or dying man is leaned against a tree and observed through binoculars. The Coen Brothers potentially reflected this scene in *No Country for Old Men*. An image

that was used on some of the posters is that of Hackman laying out bodies like you would display game after a safari.

This is a nihilistic and bloody story, just the way I like my '70s films.

LEVY-GARDNER-LAVEN présente

OLIVER REED
CANDICE BERGEN
GENE HACKMAN

dans **"LES CHAROGNARDS"**

Et avec SIMON OAKLAND·MITCHELL RYAN·L.Q.JONES
Scénario de WILLIAM NORTON et GILBERT ALEXANDER & LOU MORHEIM
Histoire de GILBERT ALEXANDER & LOU MORHEIM·Produit par LOU MORHEIM
Producteur Exécutif JULES LEVY et ARTHUR GARDNER·Réalisé par DON MEDFORD
Musique de RIZ ORTOLANI·COLOR by Deluxe   United Artists

DECONSTRUCTING HOLMES

SHERLOCK IN THE 1970s

Brian J. Robb examines the major films of the 1970s that took on the iconic figure of Sherlock Holmes, with actors as diverse as Robert Stephens, George C. Scott, Nicol Williamson and Christopher Plummer tackling the great detective.

Each decade has their own definitive screen Sherlock Holmes. While Peter Cushing, Christopher Lee and John Neville all tried out as Arthur Conan Doyle's famous consulting detective in the '60s, it was the BBC television series led by Douglas Wilmer that won the accolades. In the '80s, it was again a television version (from Granada) starring Jeremy Brett as Holmes that was considered one of the best portrayals ever. The '70s were different: several actors tried their hand at playing Holmes, but no one managed to make the part their own. Serious filmmakers who tackled Sherlock Holmes seemed intent on deconstructing the great detective, uncovering what made him tick. A quartet of '70s movies vied to be the definitive Holmes, each very different.

Billy Wilder had long been a Sherlock Holmes fan, making a deal with the Conan Doyle estate in summer 1957 for a potential movie. For almost 15 years he attempted to mount various versions, from a musical featuring Rex Harrison to straight takes with Peter O'Toole or Louis Jourdan. By the '60s, Wilder had Peter Sellers lined up to play Watson alongside O'Toole as Holmes. Wilder and Sellers didn't get on during *Kiss Me Stupid* (1964), and his participation in both movies became moot when the actor suffered a debilitating heart attack in April 1964. Wilder famously quipped: "Heart attack? You have to have a heart before you can have an attack..." Wilder was planning his Sherlock Holmes film for 1965 (with Louis Jourdan) when he embarked upon *The Fortune Cookie* (1966) to take advantage of the availability of Jack Lemmon, so his Holmes movie was postponed once again.

Finally, Wilder assigned the Holmes project to his regular scriptwriter I.A.L. Diamond, explaining he was after "a serious study of Holmes. Here is a most riveting character. A dope addict and a misogynist, yet in all the movies made about him nobody has ever explained why." In the '60s, Holmes had belonged to Wilmer and his take had been traditional, so Wilder hoped to reveal the 'real' man. "In my picture," Wilder said, "Holmes does not solve the mystery. He is deceived - Sherlock Holmes had failed to be Sherlock Holmes." Wilder's 'real' Holmes would be very different from the fictional version portrayed by Dr. Watson.

With a $10 million budget, Wilder set about casting his 'serious' Holmes. He rejected Nicol Williamson (who would play Holmes later in the decade in *The Seven-Per-Cent Solution*, 1976), hoping to find an unknown talent. Wilder found Robert Stephens who was a mainstay of Laurence Olivier's National Theatre. Stephens was early in his film career, his most recent role being in *The Prime of Miss Jean Brodie* (1969). "I thought, 'What's good enough for Larry Olivier is good enough for me'," said Wilder on the subject of casting Stephens. Wilder turned to another of Olivier's National Theatre actors for Watson with Colin Blakely. Blakely and Stephens had appeared on stage together in Peter Schaffer's 1964 play *The Royal Hunt of the Sun*, so already had a good rapport. Blakely had decent screen experience too, having appeared in *Saturday Night and Sunday Morning* (1960) as well as a run of movies in the mid '60s, from *This Sporting Life* (1963) to *The Vengeance of She* (1968).

A stretch of Baker Street was built at Pinewood (150 yards, at a cost of £80,000, took four months to construct), while scenes set in Scotland were filmed on location at Urquhart Castle on the banks of Loch Ness. Brought to Scotland in search of a missing engineer, Holmes and Watson uncover a military project to develop a new kind of submarine (disguised as the Loch Ness monster). The project is supervised by Holmes' older brother Mycroft (Christopher Lee, a former Sherlock himself, here replacing George Sanders who dropped out due to health concerns). The 30ft Nessie prop built for the movie sank into Loch Ness and remained there until its rediscovery in 2016 during a Loch Ness monster hunting expedition.

The resulting film may not have been the musical Wilder had envisaged 15 years earlier, but neither was it a straightforward Holmes film. The episodic narrative of *The Private Life of Sherlock Holmes* opens in comic vein as Holmes gets involved with a Russian ballerina who wants him to father her child, a fate he escapes by pretending to be gay much to Watson's annoyance. The arrival of an amnesiac Belgian woman (French actress Genevieve Page) at Baker Street sets Holmes and Watson on the trail of her missing husband, culminating in their escapades at Loch Ness. Along the way they tangle with mysterious monks, a troupe of strange midgets and German spies.

Both Stephens and Blakely had a troubled time working with Wilder. Stephens had been warned by Lemmon of Wilder's perfectionism and desire to direct even the slightest of movements, leaving little discretion to the actor. The long shoot - a 19 week shooting schedule became 29 weeks, one of the longest of Wilder's career - also took its toll. Stephens collapsed of nervous exhaustion and had to drop out of his next film (replaced by Alan Bates in Laurence Olivier's *Three Sisters*, 1970). Playing a melancholic Holmes caused Stephens to feel the same about his craft and career.

Although *The Private Life of Sherlock Holmes* was Wilder's 21st film, he still over shot resulting in material that didn't make the final cut, including sub-plots and minor 'cases' like 'The Case of the Upside Down Room' and flashbacks to Holmes' student days. All were ultimately deemed unnecessary for the finished film which clocked in at over two hours.

The Private Life of Sherlock Holmes is a peculiar film, a box office flop grossing just $1.5 million in the United States. Just as Holmes fails to solve his case, so Wilder failed in communicating his take on Conan Doyle's celebrated detective. The opening tale concerning the Russian ballerina was intended to indicate Wilder's view of Holmes and Watson's relationship as a homosexual love story. Wilder believed he'd not gone far enough: "I should have been more daring. I wanted to have Holmes homosexual and not admitting it to anyone, including maybe even himself. The burden of keeping it secret was the reason he took dope."

Ahead of its time, *The Private Life of Sherlock Holmes* was cited by both Steven Moffat and Mark Gatiss as influential on their conception of a modern-day Sherlock Holmes for the television series *Sherlock* (2010-17). The initial critical reception was hostile, seeming to apply Queen Victoria's

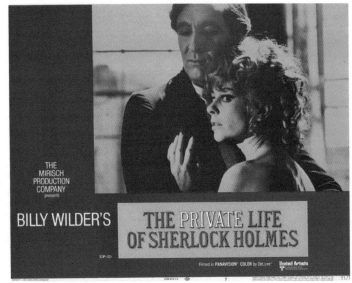

description of her journey as "long and tedious" to the film itself. Wilder's work has since come to be seen as underrated in the Holmes canon, and it launched the '70s vogue for deconstructing Baker Street's consulting detective after decades of near-reverence.

Impostor Syndrome

The next Holmes movie of the '70s explicitly succeeded, where Billy Wilder could only suggest, in portraying a love story between Holmes and Watson - that is, if *They Might Be Giants* (1971) can be considered a Sherlock Holmes movie at all...

George C. Scott is former Judge Justin Playfair, who is so traumatised by the death of his wife he becomes convinced he is Sherlock Holmes. He plays the part to perfection, including developing Holmes' much vaunted deduction capabilities, and he lives in a basement room fully converted to resemble 221B Baker Street. His brother Blevins (Lester Rawlins) wants him committed to an asylum, with the added benefit that Blevins would inherit Playfair's fortune. A psychiatrist is enlisted, who happens to be named Dr. (Mildred) Watson (Joanne Woodward), resulting in her being unwillingly co-opted into Playfair's elaborate fantasies.

Based upon James Goldman's 1961 play and shot by Anthony Harvey across late 1969 into early 1970, *They Might Be Giants* is as much a throwback screwball comedy as it is a Sherlock Holmes movie, and it confused distributors Universal. Very different to *The Private Life of Sherlock Homes*, Universal shelved its release until the summer of 1971.

While all the elements of the traditional Sherlock Holmes story are present, from George C. Scott's Victorian outfit to the following of diverse clues to solve an (ultimately non-existent) mystery, Harvey and Goldman's film was packed with strange humour (a cop, meeting Playfair in his Holmes guise, greets him as 'Mr. Rathbone') and quirky characters (played by Jack Gilford, Al Lewis, M. Emmet Walsh, and - in his film debut - F. Murray Abraham), culminating in a slapstick sequence in a supermarket (which Universal initially cut).

At heart, *They Might Be Giants* is a love story between Holmes and Watson (a female version, long pre-dating Lucy Liu in *Elementary*, 2012-19). Despite this feelgood factor, it never loses track of the fact that Playfair is a tragic figure, driven mad not just by the loss of his wife but also his experiences on the bench where, as he says of his former self: "He tried to make the world a kinder place. It drove him mad." Throughout, the amorphous figure of 'Moriarty' is used to represent the wrongs of modern life. Quirky and offbeat, *They Might Be Giants* leaves audiences with one unsolved mystery: what might George C. Scott have made of Holmes had he played it straight in a 'proper' Sherlock Holmes movie?

Shrinking Sherlock

There could be no more obvious way of deconstructing Sherlock Holmes than by subjecting the great detective to psychoanalysis. One of Wilder's rejected Holmes, Nicol Williamson, had his shot in *The Seven-Per-Cent Solution* (1976), based on the acclaimed best-selling 1974 novel by Nicholas Meyer (who also wrote the Oscar-nominated screenplay) and directed by Herbert Ross. Robert Duvall

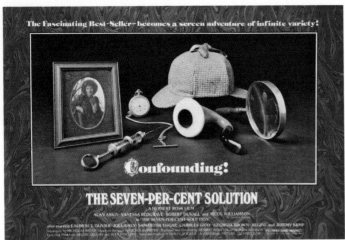

THE SEVEN-PER-CENT SOLUTION

THE SEVEN-PER-CENT SOLUTION

It's a clever, complex film, based upon a genius idea that came to Meyer during the 1972 screenwriters' strike. Writing in his memoir, 'The View from the Bridge', Meyer noted: "I had nothing better to do, so I started banging away at my long-gestating notion of a Doyle pastiche in which Sherlock Holmes met, matched wits with, and finally collaborated with Dr. Sigmund Freud. Freud cures Holmes' cocaine addiction; in return, Holmes' methodology sets Freud on the analytical path that will lead to psychoanalysis. [That] became 'The Seven-Per-Cent Solution'."

Watson, concerned about Holmes' drug addiction, contrives a fake mystery to get the detective to Vienna, Austria, where he is put under the care of Freud. While the film is an exploration of character, it still contains a mystery that needs the combined talents of Holmes, Freud and Watson to solve: Freud's patient, actress Lola Deveraux (Vanessa Redgrave), has been kidnapped. Charles Gray appears as Mycroft, Holmes' older brother, a role he would reprise in the Jeremy Brett '80s series. A dramatic steam train chase brings both mysteries - that of Deveraux and that of Holmes - to a rousing and satisfying solution.

Williamson may not have looked the part of Holmes (blonde), at least as it was traditionally conceived, but his remarkable voice certainly suited the role and his performance created a take on Holmes as a twitchy, drug-addicted yet brilliant figure that would echo through future portrayals, notably those by Brett, Benedict Cumberbatch and even Robert Downey Jr.'s more recent take. Like Wilder, Meyer was looking for the 'true' story behind Holmes, the man lost in the myth.

Shot at Pinewood and in Austria, Ross put together a professional if impersonal take on the material (he was a journeyman director, more at home with screen musicals, Neil Simon adaptations and soapy dramas than psychologically driven detective movies). Ross saw Holmes as "a little soft, a little quizzical, like Leslie Howard. There must be no preconceived [Basil] Rathbone ideas." Williamson was happy to have a second chance at Holmes, having missed out with Wilder: "This Holmes is different; below the surface there is a fractured little boy. [Holmes] is a living man to whom things are happening, not just a hat and a pipe." Although a pastiche (and definitely not a spoof), Ross suggested his affinity for the original Holmes by using the famous Sidney Paget illustrations from 'The Strand' magazine under the opening credits. As Holmes withdraws from his cocaine addiction, his hallucinations include allusions to such famous cases as 'The Speckled Band' (the Brett version featured Jeremy Kemp, the villain in *The Seven-Per-Cent Solution*), 'The Red-Headed League', and - inevitably - 'The Hound of the Baskervilles'.

The clever conceit of *The Seven-Per-Cent Solution* and makes for an unlikely but truthful Watson (he maintains the character's often overlooked limp), despite struggling to achieve a convincing English accent. Alan Arkin co-stars (also affecting an accent) as Dr. Sigmund Freud, who has two mysteries to solve - the kidnapping of a patient and the mystery at the heart of the iconic Sherlock Holmes. Like *They Might Be Giants*, Professor Moriarty (Laurence Olivier) is reconfigured, first as an all-pervasive evil then as a more human figure with a key role in Holmes' 'creation the near-perfect casting (perhaps with the exception of Duvall) won the film much critical support in the US, but British critics tended to take a dim view of the proceedings. There were plans to adapt Meyer's second Holmes pastiche novel 'The West End Horror' (1976), but the lacklustre box office performance of *The Seven-Per-Cent Solution* meant the idea was abandoned. Meyer made an interesting distinction concerning his film: "It was not a Sherlock Holmes movie. It was a film *about* Sherlock Holmes. Not the same thing."

Pastiche Versus Spoof

The difference between clever pastiche (as in *Private Life* and *Seven-Per-Cent*) and spoof is evident in the dismal Sherlock Holmes comedies of the '70s. Gene Wilder ill-advisedly followed up the Mel Brooks-directed *Young Frankenstein* (a spot-on, hilarious Universal horror pastiche) with a similar take on Sherlock Holmes, reuniting him with Madeline Kahn and Marty Feldman. Unfortunately, Wilder chose to write, direct and star in *The Adventure of Sherlock Holmes' Smarter Brother* (1975), and he was no Mel Brooks. The one bright spot is Douglas Wilmer returning as Holmes and Thorley Walters again playing Watson (he also appeared opposite Christopher Plummer in the 25-minute television version of *Silver Blaze*, 1977).

As Holmes' lesser-known brother Sigerson, Wilder

mugs his way through a plot in which he and Scotland Yard's Orville Sacker (Feldman) trace a stolen government document, encountering music hall star Jenny Hill (Kahn) and Professor Moriarty (Leo McKern). Behind the scenes, Holmes (Wilmer) offers an unseen helping hand. If Wilder had produced a pastiche of the Rathbone Holmes, he might have had something, instead he produced a noisy, self-indulgent waste of talent.

It's all the more annoying that Wilder's script is peppered with genuine Conan Doyle trivia, such as Sacker being the original name Doyle gave to Watson in 'A Study in Scarlet' (1887) and Sigerson being a Holmes' alias deployed in 'The Final Problem' (1893). Wilder had an affection for Holmes, but the scattershot humour and attempt at romance buried any Holmesian pastiche, resulting in a raucous, off-target spoof that was nonetheless critically welcomed and a box office hit in 1975.

Even worse was 1978's *The Hound of the Baskervilles* featuring Peter Cook as Holmes and Dudley Moore as Watson. Their casting might have seemed inspired in the '60s, but by the late '70s the shine had come off Cook and Moore's iconoclastic comedy. Andy Warhol associate Paul Morrissey was the unlikely director, and applying the *Carry On...* approach to Conan Doyle was a non-starter (not helped by the presence of Kenneth Williams, gurning away). Terry-Thomas was easily the best performer, and that's because he played his role (relatively) straight. Irene Handl - *Private Lives'* Mrs. Hudson - popped up, as did Max Wall, Spike Milligan and even Hammer's Dana Gillespie - suitably the film was shot at Hammer's former home of Bray Studios and Oakley Court. Terrible gags, Moore's inexplicable decision to play Watson as Welsh, and numerable other problems condemned this dog of a *Hound of the Baskervilles* to be (as described in a diary note by Kenneth Williams) a "hotch-potch of rubbish".

There is a weird blink-and-you-miss-him cameo appearance by Albert Finney in *The Adventures of Sherlock Holmes' Smarter Brother* where he turns to the camera and asks: "Is this rotten, or wonderfully brave?" In respect of both the Gene Wilder film and Pete 'n' Dud's *Hound of the Baskervilles*, the verdict is, unfortunately, 'rotten'.

There were other '70s Holmes, mainly on television. John Cleese played the role twice (*Elementary, My Dear Watson*, 1973; *The Strange Case of the End of Civilisation as We Know It*, 1977), while names like Stewart Granger (*The Hound of the Baskervilles*, 1972) and Roger Moore (*Sherlock Holmes in New York*, 1976) gave the role a go. Other '70s television Holmes included Rolf Becker, Larry Hagman (another amnesiac who thinks he's Holmes) and Geoffrey Whitehead.

Victorian Icons Collide

Murder by Decree (1979) was not the first (*A Study in Terror*, 1965) nor the last (*From Hell*, 2001) Sherlock

Holmes film to explicitly connect Holmes and Jack the Ripper, a case he could never solve as it had never been solved in reality. Christopher Plummer played the great detective for the second time (the first in 1977 television *Silver Blaze*), and he made a fine job of it, by far the most serious and, perhaps, most faithful Sherlock Holmes of the '70s.

John Hopkins' script for this UK-Canadian co-production had been inspired by *Jack the Ripper*, an idiosyncratic 1973 BBC television drama-documentary series presented by Stratford Johns and Frank Windsor as their *Z Cars/Softly, Softly* personas of Barlow and Watt. Scriptwriters Elwyn Jones and John Lloyd adapted the series into a book entitled 'The Ripper File', and it was this that gave Hopkins his source material. Although a darker take, the story was essentially the same as *A Study in Terror*, exploring the 'Royal conspiracy' which laid the Ripper's crimes at the doors of Buckingham Palace.

Plummer - a cousin of Nigel Bruce who'd played Watson to Rathbone's Holmes - wanted a second try after he was dissatisfied with his performance in *Silver Blaze*. He set out to portray a more human Holmes, a man affected by the carnage unleashed by the Ripper. Plummer also saw Holmes and Watson as being equals, with James Mason's Watson not subservient to Holmes or a blunderer in the Bruce mould. The actors, along with scriptwriter Hopkins, were keener on exploring the Holmes-Watson relationship as supportive friends than they were in the machinations of Holmes unravelling the Ripper case. There were other echoes of *A Study in Terror*: Frank Finlay reprised Inspector Lestrade from the earlier film, while Anthony Quayle (Dr. Murray in the 1965 movie) played the role of Scotland Yard head Sir Charles Warren.

Called upon by the citizenry of Whitechapel, Holmes investigates the brutal killings of several East End prostitutes. Arriving at the scene of the fourth killing, that of Catherine Eddowes, Holmes is caught up in the case despite being warned off by Warren, who later goes to the extreme of attempting to frame the detective for murder. Holmes uncovers a Masonic conspiracy to protect the son of the Prince of Wales, father of an illegitimate child whom the killer (actually killer<u>s</u>) is after.

It all culminates in a 13-minute climax in which Plummer's impassioned Holmes denounces the establishment that has allowed such gruesome crimes. The scene sees Plummer go head-to-head with John Gielgud as the Prime Minister. For one moment, it seems Holmes may be capable of bringing down this disreputable establishment. "If I could prove your complicity, I would not hesitate," rails Holmes. "I was not a party to your secret councils. Only you know to what extent you are responsible." In the event, he pledges his silence if the child is kept safe.

Plummer's Holmes is not only more human, but seems much more engaged, socially and emotionally, with the society around him than some other versions. *Murder by Decree* boasted starry support for Plummer and Mason with Genevieve Bujold, Donald Sutherland (as an oddball psychic), David Hemmings and Gielgud adding to the classy production. Costing half as much as the Billy Wilder film at $5 million, *Murder by Decree* was a more popular success, only trailing *The Seven-Per-Cent Solution* for many critics as the '70s quintessential Sherlock Holmes movie.

If the other main Sherlock Holmes films of the 1970s - *The Private Life of Sherlock Holmes*, *They Might Be Giants* and *The Seven-Per-Cent Solution* - had effectively deconstructed Holmes, it was down to Plummer as the '70s came to a close to put the character back together again before handing him on. In that he entirely succeeded, with the quintessential '80s Holmes, Jeremy Brett claiming influence from Plummer. Any actor can only inhabit Sherlock Holmes for a finite period, before passing it on to others to tackle in their own way. That's what makes the character immortal and why the screen - big and small - will always find space for a new take on Doyle's detective.

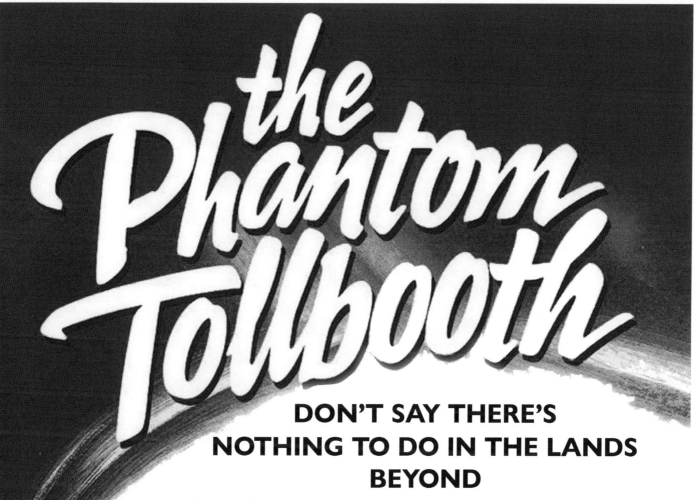

the Phantom Tollbooth

DON'T SAY THERE'S NOTHING TO DO IN THE LANDS BEYOND

Rachel Bellwoar looks back at The Phantom Tollbooth

As explained by Robert Osbourne in his introduction to the film for TCM in 2015, *The Phantom Tollbooth* (1970) was animator Chuck Jones' first and only feature-length movie. It wasn't, however, his first time adapting the work of Norton Juster. In 1966, Jones and fellow producer Les Goldman accepted the Oscar for Short Subject (Cartoon) for *The Dot and the Line*, which was based on Juster's book of the same name.

With *The Phantom Tollbooth*, Jones and co-director Abe Levitow didn't just have to contend with the challenges of adapting Juster's book for the big screen. They also had to contend with the fans whose impression of the Lands Beyond was shaped by Jules Feiffer's illustrations. Jones and Levitow don't always follow Feiffer's drawings or Juster's descriptions to the letter but, like in Victor Fleming's *The Wizard of* Oz (where Dorothy's passage into Oz was marked by changing from black-and-white to color), *The Phantom Tollbooth* marks Milo's transition into The Lands Beyond with a switch from live-action to animation.

David Monahan directed the live-action sequences. The film opens with a shot of the San Francisco skyline, then zooms in on a school (the decorations in the windows make it easy to identify), before closing in on Milo (*The Munsters*' Butch Patrick) who is sitting by a window looking absolutely bored. While it's not exactly unusual to see a kid looking bored at school, Milo's expression doesn't even change when the bell rings and, while the rest of the children rush to the door to leave, Milo lags behind.

It's at this point that viewers are exposed to the role that music will play in this film adaption. With lyrics by Norman Gimbel and music by Lee Pockriss, *Milo's Theme* plays over a montage as Milo walks home from school.

The song fulfills the same role as the omniscient narrator in Juster's story. The lyrics lament that "Milo looks at life, but he doesn't see" while Milo walks through dangerous construction sites and under storage containers without a care for his personal safety. Whether children will pick up on all this subtext is hard to say, especially since it's so early in the movie, but it would help if the music wasn't so jaunty.

In any case, as much as Milo doesn't show any interest in playing with the other kids, the first thing he does when he comes home is call his friend Ralph (June Foray, who voices multiple roles). Ralph is a new character created specifically for the movie and serves as the person who can raise the alarm if Milo doesn't come back from The Lands Beyond.

In the book, Milo comes home to find a package in his room, but in the film, it appears right after Milo hears a strange noise. It might seem like a small change, but in the book you could rationalize how the package got there by saying Milo's parents must've brought it in.

Wrapped in candy cane striped paper, like a Christmas present, Jones and Sam Rosen's screenplay is more interested in showing the tollbooth as magical than retaining some sense of reality. To that end, instead of having Milo put the tollbooth together himself, the tollbooth assembles itself, taking away Milo's ability to choose whether he wants to keep it. In the book, before Milo has even opened the package, he starts talking about returning it (Juster is comfortable with portraying Milo as a curmudgeon) but here the decision is taken out of his hands.

Other changes include the tollbooth coming with a car. In the book Milo already has one, a fact that underlines his privilege and sends a message about trying to buy happiness. There's also a map which Milo is given which, in the screen version, looks completely different from the map in the book. It's one thing to leave places out, but Dictionopolis and Digitopolis aren't in the right spots and it's not like viewers are going to rewind the movie to check the accuracy of the map (whereas you might flip back frequently to check a map in a book), so why change the layout at all?

As for the moment when Milo finally decides to drive through the tollbooth, the film definitely stretches this sequence out, and for good reason, as viewers are given the chance to revel in the effect of seeing a half-animated, half-live-action car. The tollbooth splits the screen in half, and once he gets tired of reversing, Milo joins in the fun by sticking different parts of his body into the 'cartoon half' to see what they look like animated.

In the book, Milo initially wants to go to Dictionopolis, but the film has him choosing the Castle in the Sky as his destination from the start. It's not until after he meets Faintly Macabre (Foray) that it becomes a quest, with Milo

realizing that he must save Princesses Rhyme and Reason (Patti Gilbert and Foray). The animation during this sequence is great, as instead of using their actual likenesses, the animators use letters and numbers to represent King Azaz and the Mathemagician (both voiced by Hans Confried), whose arguing got the princesses banished in the first place. Later Gimbel exposes how trivial their arguments have been by only slightly changing the lyrics to their respective anthems *Numbers Are the Only Thing That Count* and *Words in a Word*.

Another great early sequence is Milo's visit to the Doldrums, where he is almost tricked into staying by the Lethargians (all voiced by Thurl Ravenscroft), a lazy lot who believe in doing nothing all day. In the film, this sequence takes a scary turn when the Lethargians go from being harmless drunks singing a song (*Don't Say There's Nothing to Do in the Doldrums*, words and music written by Lee Pockriss and Paul Vance) to being calculating and deliberate in their attempts to force Milo to stay. Whether they really should be duplicitous (given their nature) is debatable and not necessarily true to Juster's vision, where words and names are very important, but it is effective.

Luckily, Tock the watchdog (Larry Thor) saves the day, though his character design is especially different from Feiffer's cover art. Instead of presenting Tock's body as the face of a clock (think Quart the camel in *Rudolph's Shiny New Year*), he carries a watch like the White Rabbit

in *Alice in Wonderland*. Yes, he can talk, but other than that he's presented as a normal dog which is a little disappointing. Thor's style of voicing also changes the character somewhat, causing Tock to come across as a father figure.

Because the film plays around with the order of events, Humbug (Les Tremayne) doesn't appear until much later than expected. The film also leaves out some of the context that would explain why Digitopolis is in a cave. The way Milo recites equations to get into Digitopolis is a new addition too, and it takes away from the relatability of having him admit he has trouble with math.

Alec Bing and the Valley of Sounds are both left out of the movie. The latter especially makes sense since it would've been difficult to adapt a sequence that's supposed to be silent (in that vein, when Chroma (Shepard Menken) conducts his orchestra, there's supposed to be no sound, but the film uses music anyway). In both the book and the movie Milo ultimately succeeds and the princesses are saved. With the book, however, there's an understanding that, even though the princesses are back, Aziz and the Mathemagician are still going to argue and will need help reconciling. The film is also a little too 'happily ever after', with characters like Discord (Cliff Norton) being asked to change who they are instead of being accepted. Nothing can take away from the closing montage, though, as Milo - now live-action again - goes outside to play, while his friend Ralph is teased as the next tollbooth recipient.

BORN OUT OF RAGE!
THE BROOD
by Kev Hurst

"They're her children. More exactly, the children of her rage." (Dr. Hal Raglan)

During my third year at university, I was introduced to David Cronenberg's *The Brood* (1979). Its visceral and disturbing imagery have gestated in my subconscious ever since. Much like another Cronenberg favourite of mine, *The Fly* (1986), it is a film I've continued to revisit over the years. I consider it a supreme example of his work, far more than just a 'disease-of-the-week' movie as the director himself has previously called it.

Often celebrated as one of the first high points in Cronenberg's career, *The Brood* contains the trademark tropes that defined his style and helped him 'give birth' to the body horror sub-genre (a style of horror focusing on fertility of the body alongside graphic psychological violations manifested though abnormal sex, mutations or experimental scientific methods).

The Brood was one of many Cronenberg entries to deal with this so-called 'bio terror'. Previously, he had made short experimental films, TV movies and five feature-length theatrical pictures. The first of the five was *Stereo* (1969), his masked educational film and the only really experimental arthouse movie he ever did. He would later revisit the themes from *Stereo* on a larger scale in *Scanners* (1981) and *Dead Ringers* (1988).

Crimes of the Future (1970) came next, in which Cronenberg was still in a sci-fi experimental mood. In it, he further developed the sort of themes he would employ for decades to come - themes of the body, what the body is, what it can do: the things *inside* a human being, mentally and physically. Another trope running though his work is the way the hero is usually involved in some form of scientific innovation and ends up a victim, often dying

before the end credits roll. Seth Brundle, for instance, fully transforms into a fly and is shot dead by his lover in *The Fly*; Rose is killed by an infected man on the street by the outbreak she herself began in *Rabid* (1977); Dr. Hal Raglan is killed by the offspring he created using his own 'psychoplasmics' technique in *The Brood*.

Shivers (1975) was a subversive micro-budget feature about a disgusting parasite which feeds on humans' sexual needs before turning them into zombie-controlled monsters in a futuristic high-rise building. *Rabid* followed a similar format, upping the body horror ante and casting porn star/actress Marilyn Chambers as a woman who is injured during a motorcycle accident. After receiving surgical treatment, she grows an orifice under her armpit which shoots out a phallic appendage that feeds on human blood, turning its victims rabid. It's completely bonkers and shows Cronenberg at his strangest (at least until the release of *Naked Lunch* in 1991), but it also shows him developing the auteurism he is known for today. Both *Shivers* and *Rabid* were box office hits in Canada as well as causing controversy with their subject matter. Their success led to him being granted bigger budgets for future projects. Next he took a break from body horror by following up *Rabid* with *Fast Company* (1979), a personal passion project about drag-racing starring the legendary William Smith and John Saxon. It is the only film in Cronenberg's filmography that feels very 'non-Cronenberg' due to having none of his previous trademarks. He came back with a bang in the summer of 1979 when *The Brood* graced the silver screen.

As most fans of Cronenberg will know, *The Brood* is his

most personal and cathartic piece. It is a reflective look into his own private life. At the time he was fighting for custody of his daughter as his first marriage fell apart and he believed his ex-wife was going to take their daughter away so they could live together amongst some form of cult. This troubled relationship with his ex-wife, and the emotional turmoil he suffered, led Cronenberg to create (in his own words): "my version of *Kramer .vs. Kramer.*" He has put on record his strong disdain for *Kramer .vs. Kramer* (1979), criticising its "false, fake candy" and stating: "it had unbelievable, ridiculous moments in it that, to me, are emotionally completely false." In Cronenberg's eyes, the characters of Dustin Hoffman and Meryl Streep and the situation they were in were unrealistic, unlike the characters played by Samantha Eggar and Art Hindle in *The Brood*. Cronenberg's film displayed the real horrifying nightmare - the trauma - of divorce, what it means to fight over the custody of a child. He wanted audiences to explore the anger and frustration that people truly feel when going through a divorce.

The Brood is high quality filmmaking on a low budget. It is well crafted, not like the schlock Cronenberg had made previously. It was shot in Canada during the tax shelter days, when businesses invested their surplus cash in the arts and film. It had a budget of 1.5 million Canadian dollars and was Cronenberg's most expensive feature to that point. It also marked his first step towards a more commercial style of horror.

The film sees the director using a genuinely big movie star for the first time, in this case British actor Oliver Reed. I consider it Reed's last great film until his final performance as Antonius Proximo in Ridley Scott's *Gladiator* (2000). During his '70s run, Reed starred in twenty-six feature films, some of which boasted his best screen performances, like *The Hunting Party* (1971), *The Devils* (1971), *Tommy* (1975), *Burnt Offerings* (1976) and, of course, *The Brood*.

Reed plays Dr. Hal Raglan, a well-respected psychologist and the author of a book known as 'The Shape of Rage'. He resides in his private clinic outside Toronto - the Somafree Institute of Psychoplasmics - which specialises in an unconventional therapy technique. The doctor encourages his patients to manifest their repressed fears and aggressions as physical evidence on their bodies. Their emotions appear as real, visible marks - sores, hives and other forms of skin abrasions. (Cronenberg would return to this idea again in his version of *The Fly*).

We witness psychoplasmics in action in the opening scene, where Dr. Raglan does a live demonstration with one of his patients named Mike. He encourages Mike to physicalise his emotions by doing a roleplaying-type game. The doctor assumes the part of a bully or tormenter, antagonising the patient. The procedure is a success and Mike becomes engulfed in his own fury and rage. By letting out this anger, manifesting it, he is able to reveal a number of sores all over his body which have appeared directly because of the therapy. Presumably, the patient is on the road to recovery - the hatred he feels has literally *oozed* out of his pores.

During the demonstration, Frank Carveth (Art Hindle) is in the audience. His character represents a facsimile of Cronenberg himself, a man locked in a damaging battle for custody of his daughter Candice (Cindy Hines). Frank's wife, and Candice's mother, is Nola (the wonderful Samantha Eggar, appearing in her first horror film). Nola is an extremely robust and eerie character, one of Raglan's most disturbed but vital patients. The reason Frank turned up at the demonstration was because he suspects Nola of abusing their daughter, having discovered scratches and bruises on the child's body. Frank insists that his daughter shouldn't come to the clinic to see Nola anymore. Raglan disagrees, explaining that it will interrupt Nola's therapy. Seeking legal advice, Frank is told he cannot do anything because the system always favours the mother. This leads him on a journey to find the proof he needs to show that Nola is unfit, and that Raglan is a fraud.

Frank leaves his daughter with Nola's mother Juliana (Nuala Fitzgerald). Meanwhile, Raglan conducts a therapy session with Nola, adopting the persona of Candice and asking Nola why she hit her. Nola denies it, and throughout the conversation there are hints that Nola was herself abused by her mother on a regular basis. Back at Juliana's house, Juliana investigates noises coming from the kitchen. She is attacked and beaten to death by a dwarf-like child. Shocked but unharmed, Candice is left alone in the house.

The police arrive and ask Frank to get the full story from a partly catatonic Candice. During another therapy session, Raglan assumes the persona of Barton, Nola's father. We discover he was neglectful and ignored the abuse she went through at the hands of her mother. The real Barton (Harry Beckman) returns after the murder of Juliana and tries to inform Nola of her mother's death, but is turned away by Raglan.

Meanwhile Frank invites Ruth Mayer (Susan Hogan), Candice's teacher, to dinner to talk about Candice's well-being. The meeting is cut short when Frank receives a phone call from Barton, who says he is going to get Nola out of the clinic with or without Frank's help. Frank leaves Candice with Ruth and goes to his father-in-law's home. He finds Barton killed, and encounters the dwarf-like child which drops dead right in front of him. A police autopsy reveals the dwarf's body is missing a navel, indicating no natural human birth. At this point, it becomes obvious there is a connection between Nola and the dwarf-like creatures we have seen throughout. In fact, it seems

they are killing those who have done Nola harm.

Nola is a victim too and is now being manipulated by Raglan. It is implied she doesn't know how destructive the brood are, nor that they are killing those close to her. After hearing about Nola's parents, Raglan realises their deaths coincide uncannily with Nola's therapy sessions. Could the sessions somehow have motivated the murders? Raglan closes the clinic and sends all the other patients away. Frank learns about the closure from Mike, who reveals that Nola is the only patient Raglan has kept at the clinic. Frank goes to the clinic in search of his daughter, who has been taken by the brood, and is met by Raglan.

Here, Raglan explains the truth of Nola's connection to the brood, that the killer dwarfs are in fact physical manifestations born out of her rage. Realising things have gone too far, Raglan offers to try to rescue Candice from the brood while Frank distracts Nola. Frank offers a fake reunion with Nola, but she starts to realise he is lying. She tells Frank that she would rather have Candice dead then taken away from her which, of course, makes Candice become the new target of the brood.

The Brood's final shot suggests a circular, cyclical narrative structure - the notion of something passing from generation to generation. You think it's all over when Frank and Candice leave safely from Somafree Institute, but the sudden zooming close-up of Candice's arm shows two small skin abrasions, making us wonder if the physical manifesting of fears and frustrations is going to begin all over again through the child.

Great as the film is, there are still flaws. A notable one is the too-brief running time. A whole lot is crammed into the hour-and-a-half duration - some might say *too* much. Frank's suspicion that his institutionalised wife is abusing their daughter... the legal custody battle as Frank tries to

stop Candice from seeing her mother at the clinic... his discovery that the treatment that can cause cancerous growths... the sudden violent deaths of those close to Frank... the matter of Frank's relationship with his daughter's teacher... Nola's troubled relationship with her own mother and father... plus a few subtle hints that Raglan might be sexually attracted to Nola. Also interesting is the question of why the brood kidnap Candice - we know the dwarf-like creatures respond and react to Nola's rage, yet we're never sure if they realise they have taken her daughter. Most of these threads are tied together fairly coherently by the end.

A key point in The Brood's success is the great practical effects. The prosthetics and make-up was done by effects legend Jack Young, who had worked on The Wizard of Oz and Apocalypse Now among many others. The brood dwarfs' faces and hands were made from rubber latex and look remarkably convincing. The autopsy scene with the dwarf creature on the table was in fact a child-size model made entirely out of wax. The maternal sequence where Nola reveals the birth sack growing on her outer body and tears it open looks absolutely great. It really holds up and looks as grotesque and horrifying today as it did back in 1979. It's the film's most infamous, icky and nauseating scene, and I can see why it caused an issue with the censors of the day. Originally it was cut from many prints, but was restored in the years that followed.

The Brood marked Cronenberg's first collaboration with fellow Canadian composer Howard Shore. Shore would go onto score the majority of Cronenberg's works, including Scanners, Videodrome, The Fly, Dead Ringers, M. Butterfly, Crash, eXistenZ, Spider, A History of Violence, Eastern Promises, Cosmopolis and Map to the Stars. I always feel Shore is channelling his inner Bernard Herrmann with his work on The

Brood. The use of high-pitched violins on the main theme, especially at the 0:55 seconds mark, is a blatant homage to 'The Murder Theme' from Psycho (1960). Elements of the opening theme of The Brood can be traced to Shore's other works, an obvious example being the opening theme from The Fly.

Cronenberg's 'body horror' days would seem to be over if contemporary releases like A Dangerous Method (2011) Cosmopolis (2012) and Map to the Stars (2014) are anything to go by. Still, one only has to look at his '70s run to

know he was creating a blueprint which would kickstart a whole new horror subgenre. Indeed, 'body horror' is still making a big impact in the current cinematic landscape as evidenced in films like The Human Centipede (2009), Tusk (2014), Spring (2014), Rabid (2019) and Possessor (2020). The latter was directed by Cronenberg's son, Brandon.

Overall, I think The Brood fully shaped David Cronenberg into what he would be known as for decades to come: 'The Baron of Blood'. What a title to be given! And how richly deserved it is!

THE ULTIMATE EXPERIENCE
IN INNER TERROR

DAVID CRONENBERG'S

THE BROOD

BEYOND HORROR DESIGN presents

OLIVER REED and SAMANTHA EGGAR
in DAVID CRONENBERG'S THE BROOD with ART HINDLE
and NUALA FITZGERALD HENRY BECKMAN SUSAN HOGAN CINDY HINDS
written and directed by DAVID CRONENBERG produced by CLAUDE HEROUX
executive producers VICTOR SOLNICKI and PIERRE DAVID
cinematography by MARK IRWIN music by HOWARD SHORE a MUTUAL/ELGIN INTERNATIONAL PRODUCTION

A HERO AIN'T NOTHIN' BUT A SANDWICH

by Aaron Stielstra

The '70s prospered in teen movies featuring familiar angst and coming-of-age trauma (e.g. *Summer of '42, Ode to Billy Joe*). There were also films about surviving Little League in the face of adult dysfunction (e.g. *The Bad News Bears*), or poor Robbie Benson being surrounded by grizzly outlaws (*Jory*). When youth films explored inner-city life they were often confined to the barracks of well-meaning TV movies of the week. When tackling drug themes, these movies were often handicapped by naive scripts or handled with kid gloves.

A Hero Ain't Nothin' but a Sandwich belongs to the genre of brutal adult films like *The Panic in Needle Park* and *Born to Win* which deal with heroin addiction. Its protagonist is not like some wisecracking 13-year-old you might encounter in a movie about ghetto adolescence like *Monkey Hustle, Cooley High* or a TV sitcom. During a time when the black action film was barely holding on but a comedy like *Car Wash* won popular audiences, this kind of drama was fresh and shocking. Regardless of having an almost entirely black cast, the film's vivid lead performance of Larry B. Scott as Benjie comes across with such credible force (especially as he is in every scene) that you're moved by his struggle, not subjected to pre-conditioned racial messages.

The author/playwright Alice Childress, who wrote the original novel and the screenplay, had witnessed her book being removed from high school library shelves in 1975. Benjie's story unfolds in stark enough fashion as he and a pal leave school, barely missing a random mugging of an old lady in broad daylight (a woman who turns out to be Benjie's own grandmother).

The setting is Watts, Los Angeles, and the movie benefits from director Ralph Nelson's location work, showing streets as authentic and bleak as those found in the NYC crime films of the decade. The environment - bail bonds offices, fast-food joints, abandoned buildings and rooftops converted into smoking lounges for kids selling cheap joints of "mean herb" - is a rough world. It soon encourages Benjie's use of weed and wine to include little "skin pops" for 2 dollars. The local dealer (Kevin Hooks) knows plenty about seducing kids with lessons on how to be cool. He conveniently trains his adolescent members to administer shots to new recruits like Benjie. Inevitably, Bennie becomes an addict and soon is making drops in locations as far away as Muscle Beach to pay for his habit.

Addiction movies inspire big performances that receive accolades. Here, the drug element validates Scott's contribution to the trophy chest for riveting '70s junkie characterizations, but the young actor brings a lot more. Other issues are explored: Benjie's alienated lifestyle, raised by a family of newcomers; his relationship with his teachers; his own identity as a burgeoning writer. Alongside the impressive amount of R-rated profanity (surprising for a PG-rated movie), Scott supplies his part with the magnetism of a young star and the volcanic turmoil and temperament of a young De Niro.

Rather than merely linger on the downward spiral of Benjie's addiction, the movie shows his deterioration by including Benjie's mother, Cicely Tison, and her boyfriend, Paul Winfield. Both characters are valid, interesting participants in Benjie's struggle, even if Winfield's outbursts of authority while clad in a bathrobe and holding a saxophone are often comical. At least his character is a departure from the authority stereotypes often seen scolding and ranting onscreen. These parent and guardian figures aren't relegated to the background, and this further prevents the risk of *Hero* succumbing to mushy one-dimensional melodramatics, especially as Winfield and Tyson are excellent in their parts.

Director Nelson only loses some of the movie's pace and depth when leaving the character of Benjie to inject scenes of awkward political argument between teachers. Though the actors are decent, they become pundits speaking dialogue that is too 'written', lacking in naturalness. Regardless, if the adults risk hijacking

a *hero ain't nothin' but a sandwich*

a *hero ain't nothin' but a sandwich*

the story in a few places, nothing can take away from the scenes featuring Scott. He knows the score. Benjie, realizing his own distrust of Winfield, says: "If a real dad will cut out, what do you think a step will do?" This comes just before a moment of despair where he is on his knees in a bathroom. "This ain't no jive prayer," he says. Adding to this moment is another showing Scott withdrawing in a hospital lobby with a stoic Tyson alongside. The results are some of the saddest scenes to grace '70s addiction cinema.

Later, the adult residents of a drug rehab subject a seething (though very small and tightly wound) Scott to a form of anger therapy which plays like something out of *Scared Straight!* (1978). Here, the intensity of both Scott's acting and the movie's message collectively abandon all bullshit. Despite the spectacle and controversy of watching adults scream at a kid about accepting his demons and addicted state, the documentary-style approach works effectively. And Scott's resistance can't betray the glimpse of surrender in his eyes. If there's another kid actor of the '70s to give a more lovable, tough and heartbreaking performance, I must have missed it. And there *were* some amazing child performers in the '70s - Robby Benson, Tatum O'Neal, Justin Henry in *Kramer Vs. Kramer*, the great Alfred Lutter in *Alice Doesn't Live Here Anymore...* but Larry B. Scott is a frontrunner.

The film's funky score is courtesy of flutist Hubert Laws and Tom McIntosh, whose soundtrack fails to pander to the heavy subject matter in delicate places. During an artistic montage of black-and-white photos depicting Benjie's recovery, the music and the editing complement each other without evoking that '70s style of storytelling which reminds one of the credit sequences from *The Rockford Files* or *Baretta*.

Hero accomplishes many things within the addiction movie genre. Sadly, it is an unfortunate reminder that gritty teen dramas and post-1970s movies were often deemed incompatible for mass audiences. Nowadays, the film would likely earn a studio memo to grammar-correct the title. A graphic yet chic movie like *Requiem for a Dream* (2000) doesn't carry the edge of the original Hubert Selby Jr. novel, nor does it contain much humanity. Instead, it simply bludgeons its audience with anti-drug messages and imagery. Another attempt, *Less Than Zero* (1987), is an emasculated movie adaptation of the raw Bret Easton Ellis book, more interested in its soundtrack than its content. Note how in these post '70s movies the age group never dips below 17. A very young addict like Benjie is not only fighting his addiction, he's also surviving his troubled environment amid a multitude of confusing adult figures. Amongst the foster dads, drug-dealers, social workers, rehab companions and dangerous friends in his path, Benjie remains alone to contend with himself. Will he choose a drug escape over facing harsh, adolescent reality? This isn't the crisis of an adult. Unlike an adult addict, Bennie's case is newborn and presents meager documented history of recovery.

It's a hard task for a film to cover, but Childress and Nelson keep things moving without too many interruptions of false hope. Benjie often reacts violently to this help. The movie's mostly white recovery figures, sanctimonious educators, grimy waiting rooms and the streets themselves aren't promising beacons of hope. More than what *Hero* achieves in the grit and sincerity of its performances is the grunt's-eye view of addiction told from a 13-year-old's point of view.

And that definitely "ain't no jive prayer."

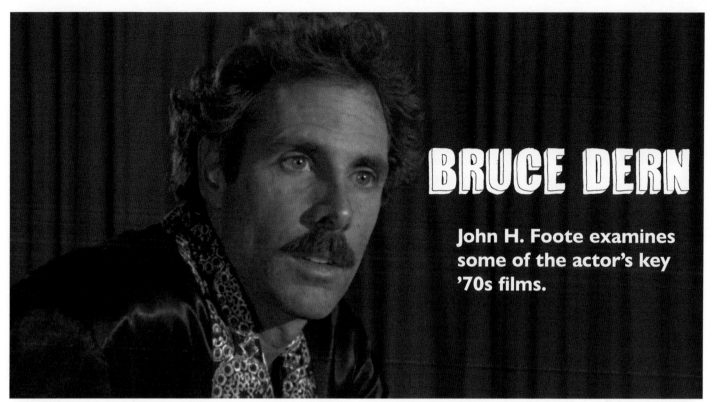

BRUCE DERN

John H. Foote examines some of the actor's key '70s films.

The first time I remember seeing Bruce Dern onscreen was as Long Hair in *The Cowboys* (1972). He radiated such danger and menace that I cringed a little every time he came on the screen - he scared the 11-year-old me. You just knew something terrible was going to happen and *he* was going to be at the centre of it all. The film sees John Wayne's character, Wil Andersen, reluctantly hiring a gang of young boys when he cannot get men to drive cattle for him. Long Hair turns up and tries to talk his way into working for Andersen, but the older man takes an instant dislike to him and sends him away (which makes Long Hair furious). Long Hair and his men follow the herd and finally come face to face with Andersen. The grizzled old cattleman gives Long Hair a terrible beating, then turns his back to march away. As Andersen walks away, he is shot in

the back and killed by Long Hair. The boys Andersen hired for the drive are terrified, but gather together to challenge Long Hair, eventually killing him (to cheers in the cinema), thereby evening the score for their beloved boss.

John Wayne had been shot in the back and killed, a cowardly move, and Bruce Dern was the one who'd done it. He instantly became the most hated man in American film.

Dern's father told him not to take the part, but the young actor was desperate for work. Moreover, this was a John Wayne film and sure to be a hit… and actors enjoy being in hits.

The day of shooting the scene, Dern found Wayne - now in his sixties - a formidable man, a tower of strength. Their fight was choreographed but, as often happens when staging fights, some realism sneaked in. The younger man was shocked by the power Wayne still possessed. "He grabbed me at one point and I was locked in place, could not move," explained Dern. "It was like fighting a goddam tree!"

Contemporary audiences might have hated him, but his performance is electrifying and unforgettable. He gives the film a huge burst of energy, however dark, and it's a satisfying moment when Andersen's boys manage to kill him, avenging the murder of their talismanic boss. From the moment Long Hair applies for the job of driving the cattle, he seems insidious. He and his fellow bad guys follow the herd and the kids until he decides it's time to make his deadly move. It was - and remains - one of the biggest shock moments in film history, and still draws a huge intake of breath at screenings. No-one can quite believe John Wayne has been shot dead by this guy!

Over the next eight years, Dern was an active force in the movie business, proving himself one of the finest actors in modern film. Fellow actors sang his praises, directors loved him and he seemed to be in everything. Yet after 1981, it was like he'd dropped off the face of the earth. His last film before his disappearance was the controversial *Tattoo* (1981) in which he and Maud Adams reportedly had real sex while shooting a scene.

Dern's work in the '70s remains the apex of his career, though it wasn't until his performance in *Nebraska* (2012) that he was nominated for a Best Actor Oscar. Taking nothing away from *Nebraska*, he was brilliant long before 2012 - in the '70s alone, his work was consistently astounding.

The year before being cast as Long Hair in *The Cowboys* he had won the prestigious National Society of Film Critics Award for Best Supporting Actor for his superb work in Jack Nicholson's first directorial effort *Drive, He Said* (1971). Avoided by audiences but embraced by critics (well, some of them), great things were said about Dern and thus he won the award. It was Nicholson who called him to deliver the news, and initially Dern thought it was a joke of some kind. Only when he detected the pride in Nicholson's voice was he finally convinced.

The two followed *Drive, He Said* with a lovely, melancholic tale of two brothers in *The King of Marvin Gardens* (1972) directed by Bob Rafelson. Dern would later be told by a well-known director who wanted him for a plum role in *The Great Gatsby* (1974) that his performance in *The King of Marvin Gardens* was the finest by an American actor he'd seen in twenty-five years. Nicholson portrays the quieter of the two brothers, while Dern is the broad and effusive one, the schemer, his mind always working. It is his scheming that costs him his life, though his careless attitude towards women doesn't help either. Dern, Nicholson and the sublime Ellen Burstyn were the leads, each elevating the work of the others. The two males drew the better notices, Dern especially. Nicholson opens the film with a shattering monologue, and we are in its quiet grip from that moment on. Convinced by his fast-talking brother Jason (Dern) to go along with a scam that turns dangerous, the younger sibling David (Nicholson) knows he should walk away, but Jason somehow - as he always has - convinces him to stick around.

Silent Running (1972) came next, a little movie that has become something of a cult classic. Set in the future, in outer space, Dern plays a botanist charged with keeping plants alive to help the fauna on whatever planet Earthmen decide to colonize. You see, Earth is dying and humans are looking for a new home. Dern's character, Freeman Lowell, is in charge of maintaining a greenhouse on a spacecraft. It's a lonely task so he has built three robots - Huey, Dewey and Louie - to keep him company. He does not connect with people, preferring the solitude of plants. When he learns his project is being shut down, he commits murder and goes rogue to keep the plants alive. The film was directed by Douglas Trumbull, the special effects genius for Stanley Kubrick on *2001 - A Space Odyssey* (1968). Again, Dern's command of the screen is outstanding and he was noticed by other directors and casting agents. His star was rising.

The Laughing Policeman (1973) gave the actor a chance to "learn what not to do on a film when you are the star", as he watched Walter Matthau make the lives of the crew

hell. "He was always great with me," explained Dern. "But man, was he a shit to the crew!" A thriller with mainstream appeal, *The Laughing Policeman* did not have enough to bring people into the cinemas. It opened and closed very fast.

When Francis Ford Coppola signed on to write *The Great Gatsby* (1974), everyone in Hollywood thought it would be a masterpiece. But it all went rather wrong in the casting. Robert Redford is especially out of place, lacking the danger and mystery needed to portray Gatsby. Other people considered for the role, like Warren Beatty, didn't have it either; nor did Nicholson... nor, in fact, did Dern! Can you imagine Dern as Gatsby? What exactly was the character into, to have experienced such a stunning rise of wealth and power? Nothing legal, that much is clear! Redford never seems underhand enough for the part - he is too 'pretty'. And the actress chosen to play Daisy is not deep enough. It takes real depth to portray a woman who pretends she doesn't have a clue what is going on around her when, in fact, she knows every move being made. A young Diane Keaton could have portrayed the role, or perhaps Jill Clayburgh... but not Mia Farrow.

Where director Jack Clayton gets his casting right is by having Dern play the bully Tom Buchanan. Sam Waterston fits in well too, portraying Daisy's cousin Nick (who befriends Gatsby and helps him and Daisy steal moments away from the brutish Tom). When Gatsby left to go to war, Daisy married into money by wedding the filthy rich Tom Buchanan. Tom, by all accounts, knows nothing but wealth and is utterly indifferent to human feeling. Watch his face when he realizes his mistress has been killed, run down in the middle of the road. There is no feeling in his eyes, only thoughts of revenge. He wrongly believes Gatsby was driving the car when, in fact, his own wife was really the one behind the wheel.

What is it about his mistress, Myrtle (Karen Black), that draws Tom to her? Sex, for sure, but being with her must be like being with a yapping dog that never stops barking. She wants, wants, wants because she knows he can give her anything and everything. Her husband suspects she is seeing someone, but never dreams it might be Tom. But it is Tom, a snake, who feeds him the false information that leads him to kill Gatsby and then himself.

A strapping man, Dern overpowers everyone on the screen with his mere presence, so great is he in the role. Redford with his toothpaste grin is no match for him, and the scene where we think they might fight is a joke because Redford's Gatsby would not stand a chance against Dern's Tom. He is physically imposing and lives with the belief that his money will always protect him from anything that might come up. As portrayed by Dern, he is a frightening man, likely a sociopath, not someone to be trifled with.

Dern received the best reviews for the film. Redford and Farrow fell flat, striking no sparks at all. For his efforts, Dern was nominated for a Golden Globe Award as Best Supporting Actor. No Oscar nomination was forthcoming, perhaps because the Supporting Actor category that year

was dominated by *The Godfather, Part II* (1974).

His performance as Big Bob in Michael Ritchie's *Smile* (1975) earned him some of the best reviews of his career, but alas no one saw the film. The same was true of the goofy romp *Won Ton Ton: The Dog Who Saved Hollywood* (1976), a spoof of Rin Tin Tin (the dog movie star from the silent era). Perhaps it was that people just did not see Dern as funny?

Black Sunday (1977) came next, and I maintain Dern deserved to be nominated for an Oscar as Best Actor for this thriller and, indeed, he should have won. As Michael J. Lander, a former POW in Vietnam, held in a cage for years, he is electrifying as a man born again into terrorism. The first time we see him, he is chained, gaunt and confessing his crimes against the Viet Cong, admitting women and children were killed and that he was sorry. Sent home in disgrace, he comes back to a wife who is afraid of him, children who do not know him, a military which casts him aside and an America he no longer recognizes. His wife leaves him, and he is at one once targeted for recruitment by the Black September terrorist group.

Dahlia (Marthe Keller) pursues him and gradually convinces him to join her in her plan to commit a terrorist

atrocity against America. Michael drives the Goodyear blimp on Sundays over the football games and has been given the job of piloting it during the Super Bowl. From it, he and Dahlia will drop a dart bomb, killing all 80,000 people at the game including President Carter.

The tension builds as the Israeli police arrive to help the FBI, and Kabakov (Robert Shaw) figures out what the target might be. A recording left by Dahlia has been found giving clues about when the strike will happen, and Kabakov pieces together the rest. Dahlia and Lander encounter numerous obstacles and, as Super Bowl Sunday approaches, it looks like they will not be able to go through with their murderous plan.

Lander melts down. He dresses in his finest military attire, medals glittering on his chest, and talks to Dahlia about what they did to him. Not just the military, but his wife and the American people. He works himself into a rage, and then, in a heartbreaking sequence, falls apart emotionally, crying to her: "I just wanted to give something to remember me by... I wanted to give this whole goddam country something to remember me by... If they can do it to me, why can I not do it to them?" He sobs, falling to the floor.

Recognizing his feelings are just as zealous as hers, she agrees to carry out the attack with him - just the two of them, without the rest of the extremists in their 'gang'. They drive to Miami and begin their preparation for the attack, knowing they will be dead the next day.

John Frankenheimer gives the film a sensational documentary look and feel, especially the scenes in Miami. The director knew what a special talent he had in Dern. No-one else was asked to play the role; no-one else auditioned. Dern was given the part on the phone by the director and they quickly became fast friends. The next time we see him after his initial confession scene, he is no longer the beaten man he was. It's as if someone lit a match inside him and he's become explosive. Wide-eyed, brandishing a rifle, he points it at Dahlia with dangerous intent. She has been away for more time than she said she would and he has been waiting for her return, slowly going mad. Dahlia understands how dangerous he is, but also knows she can control him, at least so far. It is among the best scenes Dern has ever performed, though his breakdown scene surpasses anything he has done.

Black Sunday was Paramount's tentpole film of 1977, expected to be a blockbuster. Instead, despite strong reviews - some glowing - it slipped in and out of theatres in a matter of weeks. The makers of the film, Dern and Paramount were stunned! They had worked so hard on making a startling film that was a plausible and realistic look at a terrorist attack on the United States. That it still feels plausible after 9/11 only adds to its power.

Black Sunday is an absolute American masterpiece, with Dern at the center of the hurricane.

From a POW-turned-terrorist in *Black Sunday*, he next was cast as a Vietnam veteran in *Coming Home* (1978) for director Hal Ashby. Jane Fonda, who had been very vocal about the war in Vietnam and her feelings against it, had worked hard to get a film made about the conflict. She particularly wanted to focus on the men returning home, the faceless men who came back with broken bodies and torn minds to try and put their lives back together. As producer, Fonda had a great deal to say about the casting. When Jack Nicholson, Al Pacino and Sylvester Stallone turned her down for the lead role, Dern expressed an interest in playing it. Both Ashby and Fonda felt they needed his strengths as Bob Hyde, Fonda's hawk husband who goes to fight, cannot wait to get there, but returns a broken man, cheated by everything he knows. The truth be told, neither Ashby nor Fonda saw Dern as a romantic lead, and Jon Voight was cast in the role.

When Sally's (Fonda) husband Bob goes off to combat in Vietnam, she begins to volunteer her time at the VA hospital where she encounters a guy she had gone to high school with, Luke Martin (Voight). Formerly an ace football player but now paralyzed from the waist down, Luke is a shadow of the man he was and he knows it. He makes a decision somewhere along the way not to be defined by his disability and, after the suicide of one of his friends, becomes outspoken about the war.

Sally and Luke gradually fall in love and, despite his disabilities, they are sexually active. Luke performs oral sex

on Sally and for the first time in her life she experiences an orgasm, weeping when it overtakes her body, not sure what is happening.

As much as she is in love with Luke, she does not forget about her husband. When he gets liberty in Hong Kong she flies to meet him. She is stunned at the man she sees. The war, and what he has done and seen, has changed Bob. He is no longer the gung-ho warrior that left. The cracks are showing as he breaks apart. In their hotel room, he wanders in circles talking about combat and his men.

"My men... were chopping off heads," he explains, clearly rattled, "because that is what they were into!"

Sally cannot believe what the war has done to him. She knows she'll have a lot to figure out when Bob eventually gets home. First and foremost, what to do about Luke. Luke loves her, but does not wish to be part of their marital issues, telling her he will always be her friend.

And finally Bob comes home - a very different Bob, a dangerous Bob.

He has a need to be with his men or fellow soldiers who were in the war. He sleeps with a loaded gun in his hand, and when he goes in for de-briefing, he is told about Sally's affair with Luke. Like Lander in *Black Sunday*, the military and the war have let Bob down, become something insidious and sinister, nothing like the great patriotic adventure he had hoped it would be. Returning home in tears, Bob goes to the garage and loads a rifle before entering the house.

He confesses to Sally that he knows everything: the army has tapes, pictures, he knows all. But deep in his soul, he knows also he does not wish to harm Sally, nor Luke who shows up to help disarm the situation. Still quaking with rage and shame, he refers to them as the enemy, even calling them names used as slang against the Viet Cong. As Bob bows his head in shame, Luke tells him: "I'm not the enemy... maybe the enemy is the fucking war. You don't want to kill anybody here. You've got enough ghosts to carry around."

It is an electrifying sequence which Dern dominates in every way. Three great actors giving it everything they had under the gentle direction of the masterful Hal Ashby, who so loved actors.

In the end, everything is simply too much for poor Bob Hyde. After receiving a medal for bravery, which he knows is a sham, he goes to the beach and strips down naked, carefully placing his clothes, shoes and wedding ring where they can be seen and found. And then he runs into the churning sea to be lost forever. Edited between Luke's speech to high schools, as Tim Buckley's *Once I Was* plays on the soundtrack, it a scene of astounding power and among the most moving sequences I have ever seen.

The reviews for *Coming Home* were very strong. At year's end it began winning various critics awards. Jon Voight was the big winner with awards from the Los Angeles and New York Film Critics groups, moving on to the Golden Globe and finally an Academy Award. The film was nominated for eight Academy Awards, including all six of the major categories - Best Actor (Voight), Best Actresss (Fonda), Best Director (Hal Ashby), Best Supporting Actor (Dern) and Best Supporting Actress (Penelope Milford). *Coming Home*'s biggest competition at the Oscars was Michael Cimino's *The Deer Hunter*, a film of great power and many falsehoods, which had managed to get a great deal of belief in its story, at least up to the awards. Once the lies came out after the Oscars, I question whether the film would have won anything at all.

Voight won best Actor, Fonda took best Actress, and the Best Screenplay Oscar was awarded to the writers. Dern sat by and watched Christopher Walken win his category for *The Deer Hunter*.

I cannot even begin to say how much I disagree with Walken winning, nor did I approve of *The Deer Hunter* being named Best Picture and Cimino winning Best Director. To me it feels obscene. *Coming Home* will always be my pick for the finest film of 1978, and Dern deserved his second Oscar for this film. His is a heartbreaking portrait, representative of so many of the men who came home feeling betrayed by their country, to families who did not understand them. It haunts me.

Dern closed out the '70s with a thrilled entitled *The Driver* (1978) for director Walter Hill, a little movie that provided audiences with a tight, taut story, solid performances, and was forgotten a week after seeing it. Still, Dern loved the experience and became fast friends with Ryan O'Neal during the shoot. They hoped to work together again but it never came to be.

After two strong performances in the '80s - *Middle Age Crazy* (1980), a Canadian comedy about a man turning fifty, and *Tattoo* (1981), a controversial thriller about a tattoo artist who makes a model his canvas - Dern seemed to disappear. Rumours floated about Hollywood that the frank sex scenes between Dern and Maud Adams, his co-star in *Tattoo*, had been real and not faked, which gave the film some press, but did not make it the smash they had hoped.

"It was a long stretch between the early '80s and *Nebraska*," Dern told me in 2013. Portraying the cranky old man Woody in *Nebraska* for director Alexander Payne ensured an entire new generation will know of Bruce Dern. He was superb in the film, winning the LA Film Critics Award for Best Actor and, for the first time in his career, being nominated for an Oscar as Best Actor. His career was revived and he has since been cast in movies like Quentin Tarantino's *The Hateful Eight* (2015), part of an ensemble as a racist old general. He works regularly, and I think it's safe to say one of the greatest actors of the '70s is well and truly back. Bravo Mr. Dern!

Carry On Seventies

David Michael Brown looks back at the controversial comedy series that laughed in the face of political correctness.

You can't get a more British cinematic institution than the Carry On films. Yes, we know 007 has been given the royal seal of approval but, for over 31 films, the Carry On team made the nation cackle, guffaw and giggle. Frowned upon by the critical fraternity but adored by the masses, the saucy postcard humour struck a funny bone that spanned generations. For a fleeting moment, the Carry On films *were* the British film industry.

From smutty innuendo and the stiffest upper lips to a complete disregard for authority figures, the films spoke to the working classes, especially in the way they celebrated the underdog and highlighted the pompous arrogance of the hierarchy.

From the truncheon-waving bobbies of *Carry On Sergeant* (1958) through a succession of occupation-themed films - *Carry On Nurse* (1959), *Carry On Teacher* (1959) and *Carry On Constable* (1960) - director Gerald Thomas and producer Peter Rogers set the template for a series that lasted for two decades followed by an ill-advised return in the '90s.

Sid James, Kenneth Williams and Charles Hawtrey became the faces of the series. James' devilish cackle, Williams' "Oooh Matron!" and Hawtrey's irresistibly camp "Oh, hello!" became their calling cards. The rest of the cast were a Who's Who of jovial thespians including Joan Sims, Kenneth Connor, Peter Butterworth, Hattie Jacques, Terry Scott, Bernard Bresslaw, Barbara Windsor, Jack Douglas and Jim Dale.

"The Carry On films were all about wordplay and double entendres," Dale told 'The Independent'. "I did 10 of them over six years, but it didn't feel important.

I didn't realise back then that they would be taken in by the British Museum archives as a great example of 20th-century humour!"

The purple patch of the series - which includes *Carry On Spying* (1964), *Carry On Cleo* (1964), *Carry On Screaming!* (1966), *Carry On Doctor* (1967), *Carry On Up the Khyber* (1968) and *Carry On Camping* (1969) - has truly stood the test of time. When the British Film Institute listed their ten favourite Carry On films to celebrate the 40th anniversary, many of the above were included. But only one from the '70s made the cut and that was *Carry on Matron* (1972).

The films may have been deemed vulgar, smutty and sexist, but while rewatching them it's obvious the women are in control and the men are usually floundering, quivering lapdogs at their feet. Actresses like the voluptuous series regular Valerie Leon sold an unobtainable fantasy; her hapless suitors were all mouth and no trousers.

Yes, the films aimed for the lowest common denominator whenever possible, but, depending on your proclivity for frivolous sauciness, there is still much to enjoy in the Carry On films of the '70s. So here they are, in all their politically incorrect glory...

Carry On Up the Jungle (1970)

This jungle-set travelogue saw the Carry On regulars head off on an exotic safari (in reality Pinewood Studios). Partly a parody of Hammer's 'Cavegirl' films like *One Million Years B.C.* (1966) and *Prehistoric Women* (1967) with a liberal splash of Tarzan thrown in, the film sees *Terry and June* sitcom star Terry Scott channelling Johnny

Weissmuller as the King of the Swingers.

The story follows ornithologist Professor Inigo Tinkle (comedy legend Frankie Howerd) as he heads into the African wilderness in search of the legendary Oozlum bird, a rare specimen that is said to fly in ever-decreasing circles until it disappears up its own rear end. Joining him are the irascible Sid James as the fearless (and lecherous) Bill Boosey and his slow-witted African guide Upsidasi (Bernard Bresslaw).

Boosey is there to protect the expedition but only has eyes for Lady Evelyn Bagley (Joan Sims) who financed the search. Also along for the ride - quite literally - are the Lady's maid June (Jacki Piper) and Tinkle's assistant, Claude Chumley (Kenneth Connor). Tent swapping hijinks ensue as a sex-crazed gorilla and a lost tribe of Raquel Welch-esque Amazonian cave girls, led by Hammer starlet and Carry On regular Valerie Leon, get involved in the shenanigans.

Bresslaw, who was born in Stepney, London, plays his African character in blackface. It's a stark reminder that these films are indeed from an era when comedy was a very different beast. No matter how rose-tinted our glasses are, it leaves a bad taste. The actor learned all his native orders in Swahili not realising that the extras were of Caribbean descent and did not understand a word. James, however, was born in South Africa and recognised the effort his long-time partner in crime had made and commended him for it.

Piper, who went on to make three more Carry On films, has nothing but fond memories of the shoot, especially one moment when her character is in a romantic clinch

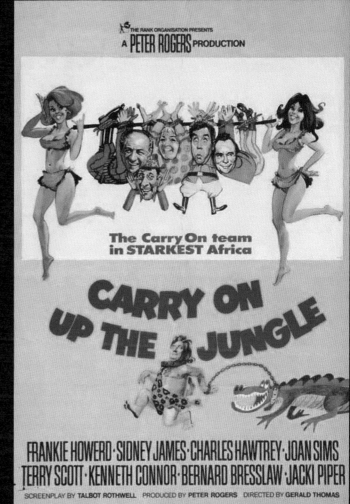

with Scott's jungle dweller. "When I was filming with Terry, he fell out of his loincloth [in the love scene by the lake] and everyone was laughing. We didn't know why, and we carried on with the scene," she reminisced to the *Retro Ladyland* blog. "We had no idea what was going on," she continued. "He didn't know... neither of us knew! So, we didn't stop... we kept going with the scene. We were aware that everyone was shaking. We couldn't think why they were laughing. It's supposed to be this beautiful tender love scene, but we didn't find out till afterwards."

Carry On Loving (1970)

Featuring the classic pairing of Sid James and Hattie Jacques as Sidney Bliss and Sophie Plummet - a faking-it married couple who run Wedded Bliss, a computer dating agency - *Carry On Loving* follows the high and lows of their patrons who live in the lovelorn suburb of Much Snogging on-the-Green.

Seduced by their promo pamphlet 'The Wit to Woo', inept marriage counsellor Percival Snooper (Kenneth Williams) becomes a client to find a wife for business reasons as he lacks personal experience. Unlucky-in-love client Terry Philpott (Terry Scott) is exasperated with the agency after a series of failed dates, including a disastrous

their actresses. *Lust for a Vampire* (1971) star Yutte Stensgaard originally appeared in this film, though her scene was cut from the finished product.

The humour is knockabout and was getting bawdier every film. The sexual revolution had started and, as well as more glimpses of naked flesh, the film features the first use of a swear word in a Carry On movie when the expletive "arse" is uttered. Some of the funniest lines are delivered by the inimitable Charles Hawtrey, as a private detective following Bliss at the behest of a jealous Plummet. They may not be married but she is jealous and wants to know what is happening between her faux-husband and one of their ex-clients played by Joan Sims.

Despite all this talent, Peter Butterworth has the best scene in what is barely more than a one-minute cameo. He plays a very strange client jokingly referred to as Dr. Crippen. He approaches Wedded Bliss to find his third wife after two unsuccessful marriages. His first wife died eating poisoned mushrooms, then his second suffered a fractured skull because - you guessed it - she "wouldn't eat the mushrooms."

Carry On Henry (1971)

"They were all simply brilliant to work on," recalled Barbara Windsor to *teletronic.co.uk.* "… and before you ask, I have to say my favourite was *Carry On Henry* because it was a period piece and I love anything to do with another period of time. It was set during the reign of Henry VIII and I got to wear one of these wonderful frocks, which was also used in the film *Anne of a Thousand Days* (1969). Some critics thought that our film was better. I agreed with 'em."

That film had starred Richard Burton and Geneviève Bujold, but *Carry On Henry* starred Sid James as the eponymous monarch who was married more times than… well, Richard Burton! Windsor wasn't the only one to pilfer from the wardrobe department of Charles Jarrott's historical drama. James wore Burton's coat from the film.

The period comedy plays very loosely with the facts, claiming that Henry VIII had, in fact, two more wives according to a manuscript recently discovered by William Cobbler. The King is portrayed as a sex-crazed despot. We join the randy Regent on his wedding night after his last wife is beheaded for failing to provide an heir. Sparks fail to fly between the king and his new spouse, the garlic-obsessed Marie of Normandy (Joan Sims), but the buxom young Bettina (Barbara Windsor) raises his ardour. He wants to to behead his new Queen, much to the exasperation of Lord Chancellor, Sir Thomas Cromwell (Kenneth Williams), his equerry Sir Roger de Loggerley (Charles Hawtrey) and Cardinal Wolsey (Terry Scott).

The film also stars Julian Holloway, the young actor who'd first appeared in *Carry on Follow That Camel* (1967) and would go on to appear in eight Carry Ons, often

meeting with the sheltered Jenny Grubb (Imogen Hassall) and her buttoned-up prim family. And timid Bertram Muffet (Richard O'Callaghan) is confused during a blind date and goes home with a model (Jacki Piper). This was O'Callaghan's first outing with the Carry On team and it's obvious from his nervy, twitchy delivery that he was cast as a replacement for Jim Dale who had left the films after his last turn as Doctor Jimmy Nookey in *Carry on Again Doctor* (1969).

The Carry On productions occasionally shared Pinewood Studios with Hammer Films and often shared

alongside James. "Sid was great," he told the *Carry On Fan blog*. "I think he evolved a persona which fitted the Carry On formula. He made the decision to stick with them, that that was what he was going to do and that's what he did! His face was like a comfortable unmade bed! You knew what you were going to get and what he was going to do."

Carry On at Your Convenience (1971)

For a series renowned for its toilet humour, *Carry On at Your Convenience* was an obvious choice, set as it was in the bathroom ceramics factory W.C. Boggs & Son. Known overseas as *Carry On Round The Bend*, the 22nd Carry On film was the first of Gerald Thomas and Peter Roger's comedies to fail at the box office, despite starring audience favourites Sid James, Kenneth Williams, Charles Hawtrey, Joan Sims, Hattie Jacques and Bernard Bresslaw.

In hindsight, its poor showing has been attributed to its depiction of the trade union movement, particularly the portrayal of the union activists who work on the production line as work-shy pedantic buffoons willing to call a strike at a minute's notice, alienating the traditional working-class audience of the series.

To be fair, the plot also failed to inspire, pitching the stubborn trade unions against W.C. Boggs (Williams) as work-shy representative Vic Spanner (Kenneth Cope) and his stooge Bernie Hulke (Bresslaw) stir up trouble, calling strikes for almost any minor incident. Then there's Lewis Boggs (Richard O'Callaghan) who wants to take the company into the future by securing a large overseas order for bidets, much to the union's consternation. Throw in James as Sid Plummer, the site foreman, and Jacques as his wife who happens to have a budgie that can predict the outcome of horse races, and then send them all on a work jolly to the British beach resort Brighton. After all, the Carry Ons were the living embodiment of those ever-so-rude postcards from the seaside.

Where many of the older Carry Ons made good use of their period trimmings (especially *Carry On Screaming* and *Carry On Up the Khyber*), *Carry On at Your Convenience* definitely looks as cheap as many of its tired U-bend gags. Jacki Piper who played Myrtle (Plummer's daughter, and the object of Bogg Jr's affection) told *Retro Ladyland* blog: "They never spent any money on the Carry Ons! The only time we ever went on location was when we did *Carry On at Your Convenience* and we went to Brighton for four days!"

Carry on Matron (1972)

After the failure of *Convenience*, Gerald Thomas and Peter Rogers decided to return the series to one of its most successful stomping grounds, the hospital. This was the fourth attempt at medical mirth after *Carry On Nurse*, *Carry On Doctor* and *Carry On Again Doctor* and was deservedly placed in the BFI Top 10.

Sid James stars as Sid Carter, the leader of a criminal gang that includes Ernie Bragg (Bernard Bresslaw), Freddy (Bill Maynard) and Sid's honest son, Cyril (Kenneth Cope). Cyril does not want a life of crime but is emotionally blackmailed by his father into going along with his scheme to rob Finisham Maternity Hospital for its stock of contraceptive pills and sell them abroad.

The cunning plan involves Cyril reluctantly disguising himself as a new female nurse to case the joint. Assumed to be one of the new student nurses who have just arrived he is assigned to share a room with the shapely blonde nurse, Susan Ball (Barbara Windsor). Unfortunately for Cyril, he also catches the lecherous eye of the hospital lothario, Dr. Prodd (Terry Scott in his last Carry On film). Meanwhile, the hospital Matron (Hattie Jacques) is dealing with a succession of difficult patients and the amorous advances of the hospital registrar (Kenneth Williams).

talking to *retroboy.co.uk*, Cope spoke about his experiences working with the Carry On team. "Jack [Piper] and Barbara [Windsor] were lovely, truly wonderful. Sid was wonderful, he really was. I got on well with Kenny [Williams] too and used to sit with him and do the crossword. I knew Bernie [Bresslaw] sociably before the Carry Ons as we used to go out together for meals. I had lunch with Hattie every day on *Matron* and she was great. Charles Hawtrey was a bit of a loner. He was wonderful on set and knew his lines but after a scene he would be sat on his own. Both Gerald [Thomas] and Peter [Rogers] were lovely men and really listened to you if you had any ideas. They both looked after you."

Carry On Abroad (1972)

The last of the classic era of the Carry On, this Brits abroad entry follows a group of holidaymakers who head to the Spanish resort of Elsbels for a four-day excursion. It was one of the last films to feature an almost full line-up of legacy stars. Sid James, Kenneth Williams, Joan Sims, Bernard Bresslaw, Barbara Windsor, Kenneth Connor, Peter Butterworth and Hattie Jacques all appeared. It also marked the final appearance for Charles Hawtrey whose alcoholism was proving problematic. June Whitfield returned to the fold in her first film since *Carry On Nurse* (1959). When the actress was asked to join, she wondered where they would travel for the shoot. The answer was the Pinewood Studio car park!

A celebration of cheap holidays and dodgy package deals, the package in question is guided by Kenneth Williams playing Stuart Farquhar. The holidaymakers include pub landlord Vic Flange (James), his wife Cora (Sims) and sassy widow Sadie Tompkins (Windsor) as the woman he really wants to be on holiday with. Other tourists include henpecked and sex-starved Stanley Blunt (Kenneth Connor) and his overbearing, prudish wife Evelyn (Whitfield); a drunken, bowler-hatted mummy's boy, Eustace Tuttle (Hawtrey); brash Scotsman Bert Conway (Jimmy Logan); young and beautiful friends Lily and Marge (Sally Geeson and Carol Hawkins respectively) who are each hoping to find a man to fall in love with; and a party of monks, including Brother Bernard (Bresslaw) a timid young monk who has difficulty sticking to his chosen path.

When they arrive on a Mediterranean island on the Costa Bomm, they find the hotel still hasn't been finished and the weather is awful. And there is something strange about the staff, played by Hattie Jacques and Peter Butterworth complete with dodgy accents. They all look very similar. Topping it all off, the weather seems to be having an adverse effect on the hotel's foundations.

A catalogue of comic calamities playing on our fears of going on that holiday where everything goes wrong, there are plenty of genuine laughs and some classic Carry

Sidney Fiddler who persuades the very doubtful Mayor (Kenneth Connor) to help to improve the image of their rundown seaside town by holding a beauty contest. But formidable Councillor Prodworthy (June Whitfield), head of the local women's liberation movement, is determined to thwart this wanton excuse to expose female flesh before it starts. Battle commences as the women's libbers attempt to sabotage the contest.

Even with James in full-on lecherous mode and Bresslaw as his hapless best, they are no match for the ladies. Especially Joan Sims as Fiddler's hotel-managing girlfriend, Barbara Windsor as a feisty biker who arrives in town to take part in the competition, and Margaret Nolan who memorably sits astride a donkey before wrestling Windsor's character over a stolen silver bikini. Despite the line-up of glamour girls on display, *Carry On Girls* hides a women's lib agenda, commenting on the furore in the press at the time about beauty pageants. It's Prodworthy's army who have the last laugh as they sabotage the catwalk. Laraine Humphrys, who played one of the contestants, recalled to *retroboy.co.uk*: "On *Girls* we were all pushed down a ramp, if you remember, during the beauty contest. They actually put fairy liquid on the ramp, so when you see us falling about that was real! It was crazy! They wouldn't

On moments. The series often played like a pantomime for adults. Repetition was the name of the game and the Carry On team were happy to recycle old gags. Again and again.

Carry On Girls (1973)

This was the first Carry On not to feature Kenneth Williams and Charles Hawtrey. Gerald Thomas may have said that the Carry On name was the star of the show, but here both of those talented performers are definitely missed.

Probably the most blatant excuse to expose naked flesh in the entire Carry On run, Sid James plays local councillor

and safety? I may be wrong, but I think that they also used real itching powder in the bikinis for that scene, so we were all scratching away like mad!"

Looking back, the actress has fond memories about her illustrious cast. "Kenny Connor was lovely, really lovely. Joan Sims was too, although she kept herself to herself. Bernie Bresslaw was great too. He was a huge man you know? Lovely though… Barbara was lovely, she really was. I saw her years later on another show and she treated me like a long-lost friend."

Carry On Dick (1974)

Who else but Sid James would play Big Dick? This spoof of the Dick Turpin legend marked the end of an era for the series for many reasons. Not only was it the final 'Hysterical Historical' period drama but it marked the last appearance by Hattie Jacques and was the final film Sid James shot before his untimely death. It was also Barbara Windsor's final proper appearance, although she did appear alongside Kenneth Williams in the movie-sized clip compilation *That's Carry On!* (1977). *Carry On Dick* also marked the last film for regular screenwriter Talbot Rothwell.

Set in 1750 England, notorious highwayman Dick Turpin (aka Big Dick) is terrorising the countryside around Upper Dencher, disguising himself as the Reverend Flasher to avoid the authorities. James, as he did in *Carry On Henry*, obviously has a ball playing a character from history.

With crime rife on the streets, King George sets up the first professional police force named the Bow Street Runners, under the command of the bellowing Sir Roger Daley (Bernard Bresslaw) and the inept Captain Desmond Fancey (Kenneth Williams) and the even more inept Sergeant Jock Strapp (Jack Douglas). Hilarity ensues as Fancey fails again and again to capture his quarry.

Turpin, along with his two partner-in-crime, Harriet (Barbara Windsor) and Tom (Peter Butterworth), hold up a coach carrying faux-French show woman Madame Desiree (Joan Sims), and her unladylike daughters, 'The Birds of Paradise.'

Carry On Girls star Laraine Humphrys played one of the 'Birds' - along with Linda Hooks, Penny Irving and Eva Reuber-Staier. Humphrys told *retroboy.co.uk*: "Well, we all got to know each other really well (the girls) and so it was nice working with them. I loved the outfits, especially where we were cherubs. However, I do remember that I fronted a protest with the director Gerry Thomas about the costume they originally proposed that we wear. It was transparent! Far too see-through! The objection obviously worked as they changed it!"

Carry On Behind (1975)

A blatant effort to revisit the glory days of *Carry On Camping* and Barbara Windsor's infamous early morning keep-fit stretches, *Carry on Behind* still manages to keep that Carry On charm, largely thanks to some familiar faces and a new addition to the team.

Kenneth Williams plays Professor Roland Crump who, along with Roman expert Anna Vooshka (Euro starlet Elke Sommer) are staying at the Riverside Caravan Park while they set up an archaeological dig at the site. Fellow holidayers include Windsor Davies, Jack Douglas, Sherrie Hewson and Carol Hawkins.

Gags fly about co-ed showers, foul-mouthed mynah birds, creaky old fossils and the campsite's randy owner. Some jokes stick and others sink like the caravan site during the film's subsiding finale. And then there is the stripper who is accidentally booked for a cabaret night. While many of the performers are getting as creaky as the humour, Sommer is a bright spark and keeps proceedings fresh and funny. Her caravan-sharing scenes with Williams

Carry on Behind

NRC

In COLOUR

STARRING

ELKE SOMMER · KENNETH WILLIAMS · BERNARD BRESSLAW · KENNETH CONNOR
JACK DOUGLAS · JOAN SIMS · WINDSOR DAVIES · PETER BUTTERWORTH · LIZ FRASER

SCREENPLAY BY DAVE FREEMAN · PRODUCED BY PETER ROGERS · DIRECTED BY GERALD THOMAS · DISTRIBUTED BY RANK FILM DISTRIBUTORS

in particular are worth the price of admission.

The film was her only performance in the series. She told *Carry On Blogging*: "I had heard about the Carry Ons. Someone suggested I should take part in one but when the offer came in for *Carry On Behind*, I was busy with other work. In the end Kenny talked me into it. I had a lovely time making that film. It was a blast. It was full of British humour, just like me! Kenny Williams was a wonderful talent and very funny. I remember they asked me what I would like and I didn't really know what to say apart from I'd seen two absolutely beautiful couches. So they sent them out, one to each home and that was my payment. I still have the couches."

Liz Fraser had appeared in three early films in the series; her re-appearance here was after a gap of twelve years. This was the last Carry On film for Bernard Bresslaw and Patsy Rowlands, leaving only a few of the regular troupe left to keep the brand name flying.

Carry on England (1976)

The beginning of the end. The heart and soul of the films had long gone. What's left is a slight facsimile of a Carry On film that thrusts female nudity to the fore. It was given a 'AA' rating in the UK and plays like a lame episode of a dodgy sitcom.

Windsor Davies had joined the series with a main role in the preceding film *Carry On Behind*, and virtually reprises his Sergeant-Major character from the BBC sitcom *It Ain't Half Hot Mum*. He is joined by Melvyn Hayes, revisiting his effeminate side-kick role. This makes *Carry on England* all too familiar - it is lazy scriptwriting and even lazier filmmaking.

The other main roles are played by established and recognisable faces including Judy Geeson and Patrick Mower (making his debut in a Carry On film) as respectively, Sergeant Tilly and willing Sergeant Len Able, the ring leaders of the sexed-up co-ed soldiers who are gunning a battalion with a wooden gun. Much to the horror of their new Captain, the 'hilariously' named Captain S. Melly (Kenneth Connor) proclaims the cold wind of change is going to blow through the camp. Joan Sims and Peter Butterworth both have small supporting roles but in terms of the legacy cast, that's it. Certain actors were obviously hired to replace familiar faces. Busty Diane Langton was an obvious Babs Windsor alternative but lacked her mischievous charm.

The story is slight at best. While training on their 'training' gun, the recruits are more interested in keeping the British end up than defending the sovereign nation especially when they are forced to sleep in 'his' and 'hers' quarters by the hapless Captain Melly. His increasingly

haphazard efforts at stopping nature from taking its course, plus Davies' histrionic delivery as Sergeant-Major 'Tiger' Bloomer, soon become tiresome. Much like the whole film.

The film was a box office failure and was pulled from most screens after only a few days. After almost two decades of success, albeit lessening in the '70s, the end was in sight for the Carry On films.

Carry on Emmannuelle (1979)

The decade ended with the nadir of the Carry On films. Throughout the '70s, the cheeky glimpse of flesh and bawdy humour had sated audiences' delectations. But now the series was being given a run for its money. The Confessions series that kicked off with *Confessions of a Window Cleaner* (1974), plus a ribald British exploitation scene which put stars like Mary Millington on the map in films like *Come Play with Me* (1977), were offering more graphic pleasures. Feeling he had to compete, Rogers spoofed Just Jaeckin's *Emmanuelle* (1974) starring Sylvia Kristel, with an extra 'n' to avoid a lawsuit. The results are a flaccid comedy that barely raises a titter, let alone a belly laugh. The cast all try in vain but Williams in particular appears ill at ease with some of the scenes he has to perform.

At the centre of this fiasco is Suzanne Danielle as Emmannuelle Prevert, the promiscuous wife of the French ambassador, Émile Prevert (Williams). She is unable to inflame passion in their relationship after an unfortunate hang-gliding entanglement with a church spire. A sexually frustrated Emmannuelle is forced to find pleasure with everyone from the Lord Chief Justice (Llewellyn Rees) to chat show host Harold Hump (Henry McGee) and the Prime Minister (Robert Dorning). But when a jealous ex-lover dishes the dirt, a scandal ensues.

Of the regulars, Jack Douglas plays Lyons the butler, Kenneth Connor is Leyland the chauffeur, Joan Sims is housekeeper Mrs. Dangle, and aged boot-boy Richmond is played by the ever-wonderful Peter Butterworth. Larry Dann plays Theodore, Emmannuelle's spurned lover, and Beryl Reid makes her Carry On debut as his mum.

And then there was Danielle. At this stage in her career, the actress had appeared in one episode of the tough-talking cop show *The Professionals* and featured as 'Woman in Men's Toilet' in *The Stud* (1978) and 'Girl at Party' in *The Wild Geese* (1978). *Carry on Emmannuelle* probably didn't elevate her in the way that a major movie role should have. She certainly injects youth and vigour into the mostly creaky older cast, but playing the lead in the worst Carry On film proves a thankless task (as it would have for *any* actress).

Unsurprisingly, the film was savaged by the critics.

The golden era of the Carry On film was well and truly over.

AN INFERIOR EASTWOOD WESTERN? YOU MUST BE KIDDING!

JOE KIDD

by Ian Taylor

On paper, *Joe Kidd* should have been a huge hit, basking in widespread popularity. Released by Malpaso (Eastwood's own company, co-launched with Irving Leonard in 1967 using profits from the Dollars trilogy), it proudly opens by announcing in big red letters that it stars 'Clint Eastwood as Joe Kidd'. In addition, it features such interesting names as Robert Duvall, John Saxon, Don Stroud and Paul Koslo. Not only that, my friends, but it is directed by John Sturges! Scripted by Elmore Leonard!! And scored by Lalo Schifrin!!!

As it turned out, it grossed $5.8 million at the box office and garnered some positive reviews such as the 'Los Angeles Times' calling it: "a concise, solidly crafted western." However, it was not a huge success and many of the attached names seemed unhappy with the results.

Perhaps some viewers dislike the way it starts like a typical Eastwood vehicle but then doesn't seem to use him as the star consistently. Clint plays a variation on his standard western antihero, in this case a former bounty hunter who has retired from that occupation but still manages to find himself in trouble with the local law. He isn't much liked by everyone,

but he doesn't much care. So far, so normal. What differs though, is that the character of Kidd constantly assesses his role and changes his allegiances. He is often a prisoner of someone or other, incarcerated some place or other, and even when free is oft-times nothing more than an observer. Sure, he can still win a fight - with guns, fists, or even a steam train at one point - but he rarely seems to call the shots. Does this make it a bad movie? Not for me, rather it is just a little bit different. In fact, if I might jump decades for a moment, it reminds me of a conversation I overheard in a VHS rental store during the early '90s. Two guys were looking at various drama and thriller video cases and one gestured to a copy of *White Hunter, Black Heart*. "Worst film Clint Eastwood's done, that is," he said. Now, if he had said: "I don't like this... I want to see Clint as an action star," I might have thought 'fair enough'. However, this guy was rubbishing the movie because it wasn't quite what he'd expected... and that's just not on. Whilst *Joe Kidd* is not quite in the same position, it strikes me that it has become underrated because Eastwood shares Main-Character-Status with at least two other stars when viewers perhaps expected him to be the one big focus. Making him a

slow-moving character who changes opinions and sides more often than his underwear probably doesn't help either. I still insist the film is worth a watch and deserves praise for a variety of reasons.

Let us firstly look at the plot, concocted by legendary novelist Elmore Leonard. Although now best remembered for his witty, gritty crime thrillers, Leonard's earliest novels of the 1950s were in fact westerns. Most of them have been filmed too, including *Hombre* (1967) and *Last Stand at Sabre River* (1997). The man didn't just have pedigree as a scribbler, he had *genre* pedigree, and the result is a script with a message and characters who are realistically shaded, not just stereotypical sketches.

Set around 1902 in Sinola, New Mexico, the story opens with retired bounty hunter Joe Kidd (Eastwood) doing time in the local jail for hunting on Indian land ("The deer didn't know where he was, and I wasn't sure either," being the most typical Eastwood witticism of the movie). However, Kidd's plight soon becomes secondary as the plight of the local Mexican community take centre stage. Whilst having his case heard in the courtroom, Kidd becomes a peripheral figure as the place is raided by revolutionary bandit Luis Chama (Saxon) and a mixture of

CLINT EASTWOOD est JOE KIDD avec JOHN SAXON, ROBERT DUVALL, DON STROUD, STELLA GARCIA, JAMES WAINWRIGHT
Musique de Lalo Schifrin, Scénario de Elmore Leonard, Réalisation de John Sturges, Production de Sidney Beckerman, Producteur Robert Daley
Technicolor·/Panavision·   Une production Universal/Malpaso C·· Distribuée par Cinema International Corporation

might think so until Harlan's posse rides into a village close to Chama's hideout and holds the villagers in the local church at gunpoint, promising to shoot five hostages unless the revolutionary surrenders. Kidd isn't impressed and changes his allegiance, thus getting lumped in with the Mexican prisoners. Now Harlan looks very much the bad guy. It is left to Kidd to aid Helen (Stella Garcia), a female hostage who is secretly Chama's lover, but Chama is happy to leave her at risk and later points out he only used her to keep warm at night. This once again makes him looks like the bad guy to a greater or lesser extent.

As the plot develops, the opportunity arises for some typical Eastwood action, with Kidd effecting an escape, saving the prisoners and joining up with Chama. Cue various gun fights, a final face-off between Kidd and Harlan, and a martyr's surrender for Chama. It's…well, really quite complicated in a simple sort of way. Some viewers might not welcome an unclearly defined line-up of heroes and villains and might be uneasy with Eastwood seemingly buffeted by the winds of fate at times. But for my money, Leonard has written something which deserves celebrating for its idiosyncrasy. This isn't the Man with No Name. Kidd might be smart and handy with both fists and guns, but he isn't a mythical super-cowboy and this isn't entirely Eastwood's film. So, going back to the overheard conversation in the video shop, I entirely accept that some readers of this magazine may prefer Clint when he plays all-powerful alpha male who is in charge at all times. But this isn't one of those roles, and that alone doesn't make it a bad movie.

So, are there any of those classic Eastwood scenes to be found? You know, those memorable moments that would always be repeated by boys in the school playground the day after a television broadcast.

Well, it's not awash with them, I freely admit, but the opening sequence in a jail cell comes close. Kidd is continually subjected to verbal pokes and prods from his cell 'mates', but simply lies back and snoozes quietly. Everyone in the audience knows he is lulling the mouthy inmates into a false sense of security, and so it comes to pass when some hot broth and the pan it was carried in are hurled into another prisoner's face. It's a neatly edited piece of retributive action. It raises a smile and reassures us that Eastwood is as cool as ever.

There is also a brilliant moment when both factions involved in the principal contretemps start shooting, with Harlan's men letting off shots with new-fangled, high-powered rifles. Everyone scatters under gunfire, searching for cover… but the tall, rangy, easy-moving figure of Clint calmly walks to the corner of a building. It speaks more loudly than any dialogue and is a fine example of Eastwood being more than an actor, more than a cowboy. Here we see this legendary actor as an iconic symbol. Say what you will, any montage of the Man from Malpaso's finest

local peasants and his men. They are protesting the fact that they and their families are being evicted from their ancestral lands.

Chama and his bandidos make off for their hideout but are soon pursued by influential landowner Frank Harlan (Duvall) and a freshly formed posse. In the first of his rather fluid stances, Eastwood's character declines to join them, but changes his mind when discovering that his own property has been raided by Chama's men.

Leonard's script doesn't make it easy to identify the bad guys… nor the good guys for that matter. But it is the grey area of villainy that is most interesting. Are Luis Chama and his band the real baddies? The audience moments really does need to include this little moment in it.

Other fun moments include a rifleman taking the time to line up a shot, getting our hero in his sights, and bringing into focus the figure of Eastwood… who takes aim right back and shoots him first. Also, the moment when Kidd escapes confinement by swinging an earthenware pot attached to a rope - slowly, slowly, slowly - above a rifle-armed guard, descending as surely as it picks up speed, until - CRASH! - it knocks the guard out and Kidd offers an amused (and amusing) little smile. Scenes like this don't necessarily proliferate, but they crop up regularly enough alongside the verbal sparring with supporting performers such as Paul Koslo and Don Stroud.

Koslo always brought an unsettling untrustworthiness to his characters and was at his busiest during the '70s, with *Vanishing Point* and *The Omega Man* already under his belt (and tough thrillers *The Stone Killer, The Laughing Policeman* and *Mr. Majestyk* to come). Stroud, meanwhile, had already come up against Eastwood memorably in Don Seigel's *Coogan's Bluff* (1968), a decent predecessor to television's *McCloud*.

In fact, when one considers that *Joe Kidd* also features the likes of Duvall and Saxon, it becomes even harder to work out why the movie isn't more popular. Duvall plays Harlan with a very confident smoothness, full of flinty stares that remove any warmth from his smug little smirks. He is a powerful and wealthy man, used to getting his own way. He doesn't mess about. Already in his 40s by this point, Duvall was an established veteran, and he nails the character. This is the man, after all, who would earn a Best Supporting Actor Oscar nomination in the same year for his role as Tom Hagen in Francis Ford Coppola's sublime *The Godfather*. Surrounded by such heavyweights and pugnacious performers as Marlon Brando, James Caan and Al Pacino, Duvall proved himself capable of competing comparably with his quietly measured interpretation of a Mafia family's lawyer. He had proved his worth long before that of course, with early television appearances at the start of the '60s and his performance as Boo Radley in the 1962 film version of *To Kill a Mockingbird*. It was mainly television for the rest of the decade (with a few notable movie credits like *The Chase, Countdown* and *The Detective*). As the '70s beckoned, Duvall's experience and quality came to the fore, earning him roles in top drawer pictures such as *True Grit* (1969), *M*A*S*H* (1970) and *THX 1138* (1971). In fact, the actor made two excellent westerns over the couple of years preceding *Joe Kidd*, the first being *Lawman* (1970), one of Michael Winner's better efforts as director, the other *The Great Northfield Minnesota Raid* (1972), Philip Kaufman's sympathetic yet grimly realistic representation of the outlaw gangs led by the Youngers and the Jameses. In the latter, Duvall played Jesse James. In fact, he is a bad guy of one type or another in both these films and was therefore well versed in villainy by the time he portrayed Harlan in *Joe Kidd*. He makes his character plausible. One can understand how Harlan has got to where he has in life. He can turn the charm on, but he can be forceful, and when it comes to the nitty gritty, he is downright ruthless. Sometimes, such characters suffer from erring too far one way, making the switch from charm to brutality too much of a tonal shift to be believable. In other cases, the surfeit charm is paltry and it beggars belief that an overtly nasty character has become a key figure in a community. Duvall's interpretation here ensures that Harlan works in a naturalistic sense. His worst side comes out most when he's away with his posse, amongst tough men.

John Saxon is lumbered with something of a Mexican stereotype, with his wide brimmed hat, bushy moustache and dialogue that is regularly overpronounced (for example "heem" instead of "him"). In one way, it comes as no surprise that Saxon, a decent man according to all those who met him, apologised for his poor representation of a Mexican character to Nosotros, the longest running Latino arts advocacy in the United States, founded by actor Ricardo Montalban. Then again, Saxon only had what he was given to work with, and Chama is written as a callous ego-tripper, even though he is fighting for his peers. That said, the unevenness which eventually sees him follow Kidd's advice, handing himself in rather then rebelling further, suggests that there were changes made to the script. In fact, Saxon later seemed to verify it. He suggested his character was more heroic and had much more depth in the original script. The actor went on to

say: "Clint needed to be the guy who dealt with all the action, so in the end, Chama was smeared with self-serving and cowardice, so it was clear who the main hero was." This is an interesting suggestion, but a little puzzling considering the amount of time within the rather talky plot that Eastwood spends eating, drinking, smoking and…well, just watching what other characters are doing. In addition, because Kidd changes his mind and switches sides on several occasions, it does little to emphasise the pure man of action. So, was there a clear difference in vision between the star and the director John Sturges?

Well, it would appear so. In a French interview in 1990, Sturges claimed that he had experienced a lot of problems with Eastwood and regretted directing him. Eastwood in turn seemed to have regretted the arrangement too, and never allowed anyone else to direct him a western again, taking the reins himself for *High Plains Drifter* (1973), *The Outlaw Josey Wales* (1976), *Pale Rider* (1985) and *Unforgiven* (1992). Certainly, each of those productions emphasised the centrality of Eastwood's role and ensured his character's epic status one way or another.

It seems odd that Sturges would struggle on a western considering his pedigree. Though most of his early films as director would be noirish thrillers, he had directed around a dozen westerns by the time he got to *Joe Kidd* including classics like *Escape from Fort Bravo* (1953), *Gunfight at the OK Corral* (1957), *The Magnificent Seven* (1960) and *Hour of the Gun* (1967), plus the triple Oscar-nominated contemporary western thriller *Bad Day at Black Rock* (1953), for which he was in the running for Best Director.

Of course, by the '70s Sturges was well known for having a more than troublesome drink problem. While making *The Eagle Has Landed*, star Michael Caine felt the director's lack of commitment and impaired ability reduced the movie far from what it might have been. Rumours abounded that Sturges was drunk on the set of *Joe Kidd* and it has been suggested that the assistant director James Fargo had to take charge of the camera more than once. If this is true (and it very well could be, since Eastwood trusted Fargo, even allowing him the big chair for *The Enforcer* in 1976), then it is a wonder Eastwood didn't take over himself, having done such good work on his directorial debut *Play Misty for Me* the previous year.

It turns out that Clint had developed symptoms akin to bronchitis at the time, which would explain his less hands-on approach and his relatively low-key characterisation. Biographer Patrick McGilligan suggested in his 1999 book 'Clint: The Life and Legend' that Eastwood was suffering from panic attacks, which seems rather unlike the great western hero but still more plausible than claims in the press that he had an allergy to horses! McGilligan also quoted Elmore Leonard regarding the difficulties with the script and director. Allegedly, Eastwood, Duvall and Saxon were all uncertain about how the title character of Kidd would come across when put together with two other strong principal characters (and presumably actors). As a result, all three performers struggled initially to work effectively together. Leonard suggested that they were all so in awe of Sturges they surrendered full authority to him and didn't question anything. Again, quite puzzling when Eastwood was an uncredited executive producer!

At the end of the day, whatever the truth of these allegations, these things tend to stick, and this writer at least feels that the negative stories from behind the scenes have resulted in *Joe Kidd* getting a worse reputation than it deserves.

The more involved storyline provided by Leonard, concerning the legal implications of land ownership and the moral battle between wealthy city builders and indigenous natives is never less than intriguing. The same goes for the underlying theme of judgement which reaches its endpoint with a nicely metaphorical fight between Eastwood and Duval in the town courthouse, with Clint's eponymous kid acting as judge, jury and executioner from no loftier a position than the judge's own seat.

The locations are all absolutely stunning, and beautifully captured. Director of Photography Bruce Surtees (who had already handled the cinematography on Eastwood vehicles *The Beguiled, Play Misty for Me* and *Dirty Harry* and would do another eight with him, up to and including *Pale Rider*) really makes the most of the gorgeous backdrops provided by the eastern Sierra Nevada range and Alabama Hills near Lone Pine, California. Whatever happens on screen, whether it be talk or action, those wonderful mountains behind the actors have enormous impact and render the images in the film truly epic. Even better, they are supported by a most wonderfully fresh and invigorating score courtesy of Lalo Schifrin. Composing since the '50s, Schifrin is still alive now and has scored well over 200 screen productions and is perhaps most strongly

associated with awesome crime caper soundtracks such as that for television's *Starsky and Hutch* and iconic movie scores such as *Bullitt* (1968) and *Enter the Dragon* (1973). He worked with Eastwood a lot - eight times over the course of twenty years between *Coogan's Bluff* and *Sudden Impact* - and one only has to watch and listen to the third Dirty Harry film *The Enforcer* (scored by Jerry Fielding) to understand just how special and identifiable Lalo's work was on the other four! And Schifrin's take on western themes is very impressive indeed, offering both light and dark - uplifting, adventurous vibes and highly suspenseful ones.

To summarise, *Joe Kidd* is not Clint Eastwood's most exciting movie, nor his most iconic or effective. It is a slow burner that builds tension well as it ponders important American themes and finds time to mix in a little humour. It doesn't feature a barnstorming powerhouse performance from the big man, but it does offer a strong ensemble effort from all three big names and an impressive supporting cast.

Go back and watch it, not as an Eastwood vehicle, but simply as a western, and you will find much of merit. It can't be called the greatest show in the West, but it doesn't deserve to be disregarded either. No Kidding.

GIMME SOME SKIN!
Black Representation in '70s Cinema
by Allen Rubinstein

We all know what Blaxploitation films are, don't we? They're a craze of the 1970s, feeding audiences a steady diet of urban detective, crime and adventure films stocked with black talent. They transposed the passion and outrage of the black power movement into wish fulfillment fantasies in the form of violence, sex and drugs. They employed a controversial mix of exploitative stereotypes and stock action tropes to give black, inner-city communities the manufactured heroes that white audiences had enjoyed for decades. That's all Blaxploitation films are, right?

If you're a fan of the likes of *Pootie Tang, Undercover Brother, Black Dynamite* or even Eddie Murphy's recent *My Name is Dolemite*, then you know that Blaxploitation films are something to laugh at. They're a relic of goofy cultural artifacts, amateur production values and badly aged attitudes. They arrive with silly titles like *Blackenstein, Slaughter's Big Rip-Off* or *Disco 9000*. Their characters dress in Halloween costumes, sporting wide-brimmed hats, multi-colored furs and leopard-skin onesies. Look, the boom mic is in the shot; isn't that hilarious?

Originally, I was prepared to write this piece about the Blaxploitation films of the '70s that *aren't* that. I would sweep aside the car chases and gunplay and examine what else rode in on the outskirts of the black cinema wave, but it soon became clear that that is far too broad a scope. Blaxploitation films

encompass westerns, horror films, historical drama, documentaries, musicals and even the (very) odd science fiction. It turns out that black filmmakers, given the chance to tell their stories, had more on their mind than pimps and hos.

Given that, what exactly is Blaxploitation? What separates a 'Blaxploitation' film from just a regular movie that happens to have black characters in it? Is it independent production? Is it the budget? In fact, the larger story of these films are a precise parallel to that of the New Hollywood cinema in the same period. A myopic film industry limping along on outdated product would grasp at anything that might bring audiences back to theaters. What *Bonnie and Clyde, The Graduate* and in particular *Easy Rider* demonstrated to filmmakers about young white audiences, *Sweet Sweetback's Baadasssss Song* and its less political cousin *Shaft* did for African-Americans. They were proof of concept. *Shaft* earned more than 40 times its budget and *Sweetback* more than 100 times, becoming the top independent hit of 1971. That's catnip to the entertainment business, which went on to release about 400 afro-centric films in the '70s alone (the '60s barely ranks a quarter of that total).

The term Blaxploitation was invented by media outlets a couple of years into the making of these films, but long before that Melvin Van Peebles, director of *Sweet Sweetback*, knew exactly what he was tapping into. "The first night in Detroit, it broke all the theater's records, and that was only on the strength of the title alone, since nobody had seen it yet. By the second day, people would take their lunch and sit through it three times. I knew that I was finally talking to my audience." This from a filmmaker who had already directed two films featuring black characters. There was a fierce hunger out there, not just for black-led stories, which had been steadily building in numbers the previous four years, but told in a particular way. Told, one might argue, in a white way, using the same stories just with a black protagonist, the cool cat with his own theme song, the person the audience wanted to be.

But it was more than that. Blaxploitation, larger than a 'genre', was both a cash-in and an opportunity. Doors were opened, and filmmakers rushed through. As is often the case, the most interesting stories came in around the edges and through cracks in the pavement, a window of creative expression through which one can catch a view of what life was like for ordinary African-Americans during this pivotal time in American history.

Not for the First Time

This had actually happened once before, under vastly different circumstances. The Race Film movement from about 1915 through the 1950s has not received much attention, more than three-quarters of these films no longer existing today, but in those thirty-five years, mostly white companies, directors and writers turned out 500 pictures for segregated black theaters in the south and midnight and matinee showings in the north. Musicals and comedies were the predominant genres, though, as with Blaxploitation, they spanned the gamut. At the peak, these movies would play in as many as 1,100 theaters around the country, until the era came to a close after World War II where soldiers of different races fought alongside one another. Black characters began to be written into mainstream American films as the industry started the process of integration.

The race films emphasized urban, middle-class education and industriousness - stressing the "improvement of the race" while pointedly avoiding depictions of poverty, racism or injustice. God knows what they would have made of the rowdy audiences of a Times Square movie theater cheering on *Sweet Sweetback*'s pornographic scenes or his shooting

corrupt police officers in the face. More than a decade after the last of the race films in 1956, consciousness in inner-city, black communities had risen and conditions had worsened. That bygone wing of the industry would have been deeply incongruous with the civil rights era. The emerging black film-watchers clearly wanted to see not only their faces, but the source of their pain reflected on the screen, even if in a deeply distorted form. In the movies, they got to win, to be powerful, to solve intractable problems with a little hand-to-hand combat and the force of their personality.

Not always though. Sprinkled throughout the period, there's a complex patchwork of stories where an honest attempt was made to depict life amongst an oppressed minority in modern day America. What did they show through that window of opportunity? For starters, skin.

It's there in every film - the hands connecting, slapping, sliding and bumping. They're gestures of family and community, joy and affection, congratulations and admiration, of righteousness and alliance. They're about having skin in the game, a stake in one another, an identification through their mutual struggle, their shared experience surviving by the skin of their teeth. This was what audiences were clamoring for and what filmmakers delivered - black skin and plenty of it.

All About the Skin

If there's any distinction between New Hollywood films and the black equivalent, it's about the wandering. Black people weren't. The movement politics of the '60s wrapped itself around, well, movement, over to that shining city *just* over the hill in the distance. They wanted a higher calling and a transformed world, and as they discovered the limits to their power, their avatars on screen just kept wandering aimlessly, looking for purpose. Black people did not need to wander to discover their lack of power. They couldn't wander if they wanted to.

It may sound strange to say about a period immediately following the civil rights era and right in the epicenter of black power and Panther politics. Legal segregation

was ending, a process that started with Brown vs. the Board of Education in 1954 and moved slowly over the following decade. A string of victories during the Johnson administration - The Civil Rights Act of 1964, Voting Rights Act of 1965, Loving .v. Virginia in 1967 and the Fair Housing Act of 1968 - effectively closed the door on legal apartheid in the United States. In truth though, Jim Crow laws had largely completed their work by then. The races lived, worked and functioned separately, and capitalism could take up enforcement of the social order through banking, real estate and insurance institutions.

The films I'm about to discuss, on the banal side, are really just about people, ordinary human beings who have an arbitrary difference of skin tone. The characters want to raise their families in safety, put in a day's work with something to show for it, and feel a sense of dignity and agency in their lives. At the same time, nearly all of the films are about the ghetto. White people had fled the race-mixed

energy of America's cities for suburban landscapes where blacks were expressly forbidden. What was left behind was deep, deep neglect. You can see documentary footage of these regions that shows how bad things were - streets so trash strewn and worn down they may as well have survived an enemy bombing. In the opening of *Halls of Anger* (1970), a pre-*Shaft* portrait of an all-black school where thirty-odd white students are bussed in by court order, the camera glides past graffiti scrawling "black power", "soul power", "get whitey" and "Panthers".

But *Halls of Anger*, made by white people and starring the poor man's Poitier, Calvin Lockhart, feels contrived and artificial despite a handful of strong moments and one of the first screen performances of baby-faced Jeff Bridges (he's a natural from the get go). By contrast, Gordon Parks, Jr, director of *Super Fly* (1972) and son of the filmmaker who made *Shaft* brings us the most vivid depiction of the

ghetto on film, *Aaron Love Angela* (1975).

This story is a portrayal of young love in the reality of segregated urban life (and, as Angela is Puerto Rican, one of the only of these films that includes an ethnicity besides black and white). Every wall and staircase has the texture of age and grime, years of densely populated traffic aging each railing and scrap of wallpaper. The titular romantic couple find their bliss in a room of a decaying abandoned building where they cover a filthy mattress with soiled sheets and cook meals on a camping stove stolen from Aaron's father. There, they have their own experience of skin with one another before a scam-the-mob subplot sidetracks their sweet story.

Aaron Loves Angela is one of the numerous black coming-of-age stories dotting the decade with kids and teenagers who grew up knowing little beyond the squalor of Harlem or similar regions. A second, *Cooley High*, directed by Michael Schultz in 1975, bleeds authenticity from every frame. It's a prime example of how to depict hard living without overwhelming the story with misery or victimhood. Glynn Turman plays Preach, a high school student who, the end card tells us, went on to become a Hollywood scriptwriter. Preach is a stand-in for the writer of *Cooley High*, Eric Monte, who made a big impression on sitcom giant Norman Lear by creating George and Louise Jefferson in his very first *All in the Family* script. He went on to develop and lead the writing staff of *Good Times* and the show based on *Cooley High*, *What's Happening!* Shortly thereafter, Monte sued Lear for adequate credit and compensation

COLUMBIA PICTURES Presents **AARON LOVES ANGELA** Starring MOSES GUNN · KEVIN HOOKS · ERNESTINE JACKSON
Introducing IRENE CARA · ROBERT HOOKS as BEAU · a ROBERT J. ANDERSON/GORDON PARKS, JR./LLOYD S. GILMOUR, JR. film
Written by GERALD SANFORD   Music by JOSE FELICIANO and JANNA MERLYN FELICIANO   Songs Performed by JOSE FELICIANO
Producer ROBERT J. ANDERSON   Director GORDON PARKS, JR.   [R] RESTRICTED   *Special Guest Appearance by JOSE FELICIANO and WALT FRAZIER   Columbia Pictures

for creating these shows (and won), effectively ending his entertainment career.

Cooley High has better writing than all that breakthrough television - filled with nuance, detail and subtle character building minus the regurgitated wisecracks and catchphrases. It's a record of how being raised in the impoverished Cabrini-Green Housing project in Chicago formed Eric Monte into a cultural leader. Preach and his friends are

scamps who pour a sip of their "wine" (cheap beer) on the ground for the brothers that are dead and in jail. They shoplift, cut classes, jump the subway turnstiles and make out with girls in dilapidated hallways. The boys' parents hold down several jobs apiece allowing their children to lie to them about their activities. There are several sequences involving street prostitutes, including when the gang pretend to be police to steal money so they can make out with

of his best friend Cochise after a misunderstanding about an arrest at the center of the film results in his friend's murder. "There are no tomorrows; there is no yesterday. We live for today." (Cochise is played by Laurence Hilton-Jacobs, best known as Freddie 'Boom Boom' Washington in *Welcome Back Kotter*, in one of his three starring roles here - the others being *Claudine* and *Youngblood*. His talent is wasted in sitcoms.) We then leave Preach in freeze frame running toward his future. The depth and weight of these moments in a film about carefree teenagers is striking, highlighting the space between the life experience of middle-class white filmmakers putting out the likes of *American Graffiti* and what black people faced in their lives day in and day out.

Practically a sister film in 1975, *Cornbread, Earl and Me* stars a thirteen-year-old Laurence Fishburne, already acting his heart out, as Wilford, a boy who witnesses an accidental police shooting of neighborhood athletic hero Cornbread. The police are in a foot chase with an actual black criminal wearing a hoodie in a heavy rain, and mistaking Cornbread for him, they shoot him dead. After a beautiful first-act build up to the fatal incident, the bulk of the runtime shows the police cover-up, closing ranks behind one another, harassing witnesses, threatening children with racial epithets and ultimately lying on the stand.

Basically, *Cornbread* plants its feet on a graveled tenement rooftop and screams out: "NOTHING HAS CHANGED!" The only thing we know now that African-Americans have always known is how much worse it was than the film depicts. *Cornbread* wraps up its story with a fantasy of justice as Fishburne earns his manhood by telling the truth at the inquest. In reality, there never would have been an inquest, public outrage notwithstanding. Spike Lee should re-release the film after attaching nine minutes of Derek Chauvin kneeling on George Floyd's neck.

Among the films in this survey, only *Cooley High* and a pretty weak entry called *Together Brothers* (1974) have a less-than-awful portrayal of the police, as they are able to show "a few good apples" among the culture of blind racism. Otherwise, the cops are a menace. Over and over, whether they show up as characters in the story or are simply mentioned offhand, the community collectively loathes and fears this institution that has the power to harass, threaten, wound and murder them for whatever reason they deem fit. You can trace the roots of that bitterness back through the period's historical films and those

more girls in a Godzilla movie. None of these scenes carry any judgment. The film does what a great autobiographical story must do, being simultaneously specific and universal, the simple struggle to thrive in trying circumstances.

Preach is a poet, and he recites pieces he's written several times in the story, most notably at the funeral

set in the southern states where the characters are vividly aware that law enforcement can act on them with absolute impunity. There's a deep irony to see such a vein of anger against police in an artistic movement that began with a 'good cop' action film. Of course, beyond the obvious reasons to portray this antagonistic relationship on screen, the police are more cinematic and directly in contact with the community in ways that city councils, school boards and realtors associations are not.

With that in mind, by the time *Youngblood* came to theaters in 1978, the black coming of age drama appears to have hardened considerably. There are gangs to join in this hard-scrabble culture, run as extra-legal support and protection groups. (contrarily, *The River Niger* (1976) shows a street gang with a quixotic black power posture and little planning to back up their zeal for revolution. There are no such pretensions here). The gang, called the Kingsmen, spends a lot of time drinking, beating up rival gang members, and abusing each other, but when they lose a member to smack, the hunt is on for the dope pushers peddling junk in the 'hood. Unbeknownst to them, the main supplier is the conservative, business-suited older brother that protagonist Youngblood looks up to as a success story.

The story is a bit contrived, but there are few '60s-fed liberal illusions about these characters' lot in life; no lovely romance to offset the reality. Kids get in trouble at school when they're caught with a gun they found; a stick and stone fight turns into a knife fight until someone gets shot; young men shoot up in public restrooms. Family, school and their environment have failed them, and these gangs really do seem like the best of these young recruits' limited options in life.

How they Made It Through

Right now you might be thinking, "If this is media representation of black people, it's no doubt why America was ready for *The Cosby Show*." While that's fair, one thing that comes across in these films is that the characters are more than their circumstances. I wouldn't exactly say they offer up a ray of hope, but what they do show is people with tremendous strength, resilience and character. The deaths that frame the narratives seem almost beside the point to the living, and if their struggles have taken a toll anywhere, it's usually seated in a parental character like Preach's exhausted mother or Aaron's father in

Aaron Loves Angela, lost in alcohol and old football fantasies, despairing about the loss of his wife and their life in poverty. Far more common though are individuals meeting trials with determination, calling forward allies, forming lasting bonds that keep a community bound in strength.

The perfect demonstration comes in the form of *Claudine* (1974), directed by John Berry with writing by Tina and Lester Pine. It's one of the few films I'm addressing here both written and directed by white people, but you'd be hard-pressed to find more grace under pressure than this family. Diahann Carroll is the titular single mother with "six kids in four rooms" who dates and weds garbage man Rupert "Roop" Marshall played by prime James Earl Jones. In the space of the movie, she deals with Rupert's fight or flight panic, welfare rules that insist she stay single or risk losing benefits, the growing political activism of her eldest son and the surprise pregnancy of her eldest daughter. Throughout, she never stops being Diahann Carroll. Check out her response to Roop when he asks her how she ended up with six kids: "Well, haven't you heard about us ignorant black bitches always got to be layin' up with some dude grinding out them babies for the taxpayers to take care of? I get thirty bucks a piece for them kids, you know? I'm living like a queen… I get that shit all the time from the welfare, always asking me to apologize for my kids. You know what? I don't have

to explain that to nobody. Now you just pushed the wrong button." James Earl Jones, never better, has to do some fast talking after that speech to keep his date with Claudine from going off the rails. The film unquestionably has some of the best dialogue here, portraying Claudine as flawed, tired and human, but also warm, level-headed and as capable of being a poor mother of six as anyone is likely to be.

Claudine's examination of the destructive nature of bureaucracy is a consistent running theme across the board. Did government agencies ever really make this many house calls? A welfare worker also comes to visit in *Cornbread, Earl and Me*, this time encouraging the mother to lie for her benefits instead of trying to catch her cheating. Child Social Services drop by in *Youngblood*; Unemployment comes calling in Michael Schultz and Joel Schumacher's *Car Wash*; and an IRS agent pops in on Richard Pryor to count his dependents in one scene of Paul and Leonard Schrader's *Blue Collar*. In white cinema, if there's an example of this (when white cinema even acknowledges poverty) outside of 2017's *The Florida*

52

Project, I can't think of it.

The theme brings us back to the wider picture, which boiled down is black Americans versus the United States. Even if you were to take out all the examples of direct, toxic racism in this group of movies, you'd still see a culture largely excluded from mainstream society. By comparison, I'll mention two outstanding British films that are some of the earliest from their industry to feature a black cast - Horace Ove's *Pressure* (1976) and Anthony Simmon's *Black Joy* (1977). Both are set among immigrant communities, Guyana and Trinidad respectively, exactly where you would expect to experience a sense of separation and alienation from the country they've adopted, yet these films are nearly indistinguishable from their American counterparts. They cover exactly the same ground - abusive, lying police, shoddy job prospects, government indifference, targeted hostility from the general population, worn out grown-ups and the combination of increasing political radicalization and the sense of futility that accompanies radical political action against a society entrenched in centuries-old racism. It's a vision of a people kidnapped in their own homes, with little choice but to occupy space in a country where they are not welcome.

And the Rest

Believe it or not, I've still only skimmed the surface of the wealth of these films about ordinary black life during the '70s. There are three rich family dramas all derived from stage plays - *Black Girl* (1972) directed by Ossie Davis, *Five on the Black Hand Side* (1973) and *The River Niger* (1976), a stunning piece of working-class drama starring James Earl Jones. Those go much deeper into intergenerational and gender role issues that black people faced. There are four seminal films created via the "L.A. Rebellion" a group of black UCLA film grads who banded together to create a their own African-American-centric film language outside of Hollywood. This group - *Bush Mama, Emma Mae, Passing Through* and *Killer of Sheep* - seem to distill aspects of everything I've discussed above with an artistic daring and vigor that many of the other films lack. There are some mid-career Sidney Poitier pictures, comedies and dramas, as he tried his best to evolve with the times. There's even *Georgia, Georgia* (1972), a fragmentary drama with a screenplay written by legendary poet laureate Maya Angelou. To all of that, add more than twenty films I have yet to find a copy of, some of them probably lost forever.

Finally, as their New Hollywood contemporaries also learned, what can be given can be taken away. When it was discovered that black audiences accounted for up to a third of the crowds that paid to see the likes of *Jaws, Star Wars* and subsequent big-ticket spectacles, it seemed less important to the bottom line to create separate media specifically for inner-city crowds. The release of black films declined precipitously, leaking through in short bursts like the Spike Lee breakthrough in the mid-'80s, the 'hood films of the early '90s or the more recent spate of historical re-enactments. Plenty of black films have been part of the mix in theaters since the '70s, growing as a demographic niche in a fragmented market, but we'll truly never again see the free-for-all environment that allowed such fire and passion to burn into reels of celluloid.

That environment happened at a vital time in the history of race and race relations in America, and thanks to an unprecedented creative windfall, we now have a vast record of what was happening throughout all that in neglected urban areas. What they dreamed of; whom they loved and what they lost. When you consider that this sizeable collection is actually the exception to what was considered Blaxploitation, you start to understand how profound a shift this was for black filmmakers, writers and actors to be able to tell their stories. They wanted to show the world how deep their skin goes and they succeeded. That they managed to do so on their terms, and with so consistent and unified a voice and vision, is a historical gift and a joy to behold.

Caricatures by Aaron Stielstra

Samantha Eggar in *The Brood* (1979)
(pg.18)

Paul Koslo in *Joe Kidd* (1972)
(pg. 41)

Larry B. Scott in *A Hero Ain't Nothin' but a Sandwich* (1978)
(pg. 22)

Gene Hackman in *The Hunting Party* (1971)
(pg. 5)

Dr. Andrew C. Webber re-appraises Robert Altman's California Split (with a little help from Pauline Kael).

Make a list of great film makers and it won't be long before you've included Robert Altman, the maverick outsider director of such '70s classics as *MASH* (1970), *McCabe and Mrs. Miller* (1971), *The Long Goodbye* (1973) and *Nashville* (1975). He also made great films in subsequent decades, including the brilliant Raymond Carver adaptation *Short Cuts* (1993) and the costume drama *Gosford Park (2001)*. However, the less said about his 1980 Robin Williams starring musical version of *Popeye* the better.

In its first season of films post lockdown in 2021, the BFI in London made Altman the focus of an extensive retrospective. His films about communities and the messiness of living remind us of how we might have lived pre-Covid - how much being in isolation from each other seems to be in direct contradiction to our need to socialise, our need to fall in out of love and constantly, to make errors in our choices which we then try to rectify. He also reminds us that comedy and tragedy are never far away from our lives and both can bring out the best and worst in us.

In his best films (*McCabe and Mrs. Miller* and *Nashville,* for example) there's a palpable sense of place and lives being lived. His semi-improvised performances, superb use of music, and jazzy (almost stoned) editing style - coupled with his innovative multi-tracked dialogue recording - all give viewers a sense of verisimilitude. In Altman's films, the viewer often feels like they've just arrived in the middle of a conversation which they have only partially overheard and will probably leave long before it's over. *California Split* (1974) was one of the very first films to be mixed in stereo and recorded using eight track sound and, whilst it is overshadowed somewhat by Altman's follow up *Nashville* (which extended the remit to include a huge cast, epic running time and an innovative multi-strand narrative), it remains an impressive work which remains tantalisingly hard to get hold of on DVD in the UK. I had seen it only once before on TV in the late '70s and then lost track of it.

California Split is a loose-limbed, semi-improvised comedy that fits nicely into the sub-genre of 'card player gambling movies', owing much to films like Norman

Jewison's *The Cincinatti Kid* (1965) and a key influence upon Karel Reisz' Dostoyevsky adaptation (yes, you read that right) *The Gambler* starring James Caan, which came out in 1975 (and was remade in 2014 by Rupert Wyatt and featured Mark Wahlberg). The little-seen 1998 John Dahl movie *Rounders* (starring a very youthful Ed Norton and Matt Damon) and *Mississippi Grind* (2015) with Ryan Reynolds are contemporary takes on the genre, though the Altman film is far superior to both. It drifts along nicely and is sometimes funny (Gould's constant stream of invective is both exhausting and hilarious) and sometimes tender. The locations are shot with a wintry beauty by first-time cinematographer Paul Lohmann (who also photographed *Nashville* before going on to work for Mel Brooks on *Silent Movie* in 1976 and *High Anxiety* in 1977), especially a trip to Reno in the last section of the film and, whilst it's not a 'buddy movie' per se, it does paint a vivid picture of the friendship between these two itinerant male gamblers for whom there is nothing that cannot be bet upon (including, even, the names of Snow White's seven dwarfs).

Starring in *California Split* is an almost never-better Elliott Gould. The world was a better place when it had stars like him on screen - in the '70s he also made, amongst many others, *A Bridge Too Far* (1977) and *Capricorn One* and *The Silent Partner* (both 1978). Perhaps his oddest casting, however, was in Ingmar Bergman's *The Touch* (1971), another of those 'did I read that right?' moments. *California Split* also boasts George Segal, an interesting actor who said about himself that he could appear bland even if his performances were anything but - see, for example, *The Hot Rock* (1972) or *Fun with Dick and Jane* and *Rollercoaster* (both 1977). Gould had been used by Altman previously in *MASH* and *The Long Goodbye* (he went on to provide brief cameos as himself in *Nashville* and *The Player* too). He was also a big hit with *The Muppets,* somewhat surprisingly. This was his only pairing with Segal and the only time Segal worked with Altman.

Also making an impact is Ann Prentiss in the role of Barbara, Gould's hooker 'girlfriend' (there were a lot of these in the '70s). Prentiss unfortunately only appeared in a few movies before drifting into the world of TV and finally jail (she got 19 years for an assault against her own father) where she died in 2010, aged 70. Her sister Paula (who was married to that other 'Man-of-the-'70s' Richard Benjamin) had a key role in another great '70s movie, *The Parallax View* (1974) from director Alan J. Pakula. Also in the mix is the rather good Gwen Welles, who Altman would use again in *Nashville* (her humiliating striptease sequence being one of *that* film's many highlights). In real life, she died

tragically young - bowel cancer claimed her at the age of 42. It's worth noting that the movie is dedicated 'To Barbara', in reference to the actress Barbara Ruick, who plays a Reno barmaid (and who was married to composer John Willams). Ruick died while the film was being shot, and it's things like that which make you can realise *California Split* might well have had the makings of a tragedy, rendering its lightness of touch all the more impressive.

New Yorker film critic Pauline Kael (the 'go-to' critic when wanting to find out more about how Hollywood films were received upon their released in the '70s and '80s) described her feelings about Altman's *Nashville* thus: "At Robert Altman's new film.... you don't get drunk on images, you're not overpowered - you get elated... I sat there smiling at the screen in complete happiness. It's a pure emotional high and you don't come down when the picture is over; you take it with you." She could easily have been describing <u>my</u> feelings as I stepped out of the Ultimate Picture Palace onto Cowley Road in Oxford on a warm Sunday afternoon in June having just seen *California Split* on the big screen for the first time in over 40 years.

California Split leaves you feeling like you've bumped into an old friend you haven't seen for decades and spent the evening rolling back the years.

Free wheelin' never felt so good.
Pauline Kael was right - as ever.

SLEUTH

by
Peter Sawford

The 1970s was the first full decade after the shackles of the restrictive Production Code had been thrown off. The Code had existed since 1934 and, although largely ignored and increasingly difficult to enforce, it was still very much in evidence throughout the '60s. It was finally abandoned in 1968 when the Motion Picture Association of America introduced a new ratings system.

The '70s was also the first full decade after the old studio system crumbled and a new breed of independent producers and directors were given the freedom to express themselves and make the sort of films they wanted to make, not what the studios told them.

This brought the likes of Scorsese, Coppola, De Palma, Spielberg and Lucas to the fore and led to an explosion of films such as *The Godfather*, *Jaws*, *The French Connection*, *Taxi Driver* and *Apocalypse Now*. Such films would previously have been denied a licence or subjected to so many cuts they'd be unrecognizable as the films we know and love

And yet, for me, the best film to come out of the decade was a two-handed stage adaptation which combined the skills of two great actors and a great director. A film that could have been made, with slight adjustment, during the Production Code and studio system era. A film with no sex, relatively little violence, extremely wordy, but endlessly watchable and always enjoyable.

As a stage play, *Sleuth* had enjoyed a hugely successful Broadway run. Written by Anthony Shaffer, it opened on November 12th, 1970, and starred Anthony Quayle as Andrew Wyke and Keith Baxter as Milo Tindle. It was a huge hit, winning the Tony Award in 1971 for Best Play and eventually running for 1,222 performances. With such success behind it, it was obvious a cinematic version would be attempted and, in 1972, it was adapted for the big screen with two of England's finest filling in the lead roles and one of Hollywood's greatest directors handling things behind the camera.

The premise is deadly simple. Andrew Wyke (Laurence Olivier) is a successful writer of crime fiction. His fictional character St. John Lord Merridew is a much beloved fighter of crime in the class of Hercule Poirot and Lord Peter Wimsey. Andrew lives in a large country house which he's filled over the years with hundreds of games, toys and automata.

Milo Tindle (Michael Caine) is a second-generation Italian who owns two hairdressing salons, one in London one in Brighton. He is having an affair with a lady named Marguerite, who just happens to be Andrew's wife.

Andrew invites Milo to his house on the pretext of settling the issue of Marguerite once and for all, but instead intends to humiliate Milo to teach him a lesson His plan starts to unravel when Inspector Doppler turns up the next evening to investigate the murder of Milo and despite Andrew's protestations that it was just a game and that Milo is alive and well, the copper finds plenty o evidence to the contrary.

Andrew Wyke is a thoroughly dislikeable character from the word go. Privileged, rich and a snob of the highest order, he looks down his nose at almost everyone, especially "jumped up pantry boys who don't know their place" (as he describes Milo). Although he doesn't really love Marguerite any more, the thought of losing her to anyone is abhorrent, a slur on his perceived manhood.

Olivier is excellent as the overbearing, pompous lord-of-all-he-surveys. He draws on his performance as Archie Rice in *The Entertainer*. In many ways, Wyke could be viewed as the bastard brother of Archie; a brother who has made good against the odds, and has no intention of ever going back to - or being reminded of - his roots.

Olivier creates a character of extraordinary arrogance, who believes he is above the law because of his position. He has no understanding of the struggles people like Milo have to contend with. His pampered existence has blinded him to the realities of life. Olivier inhabits the role to such an extent that even when he badly cuts his hand in one scene he continues as if nothing has happened.

And yet, as the story unfolds, it's difficult not to start to sympathise with Andrew as events spin wildly out of his control. He demonstrates rising frustration at Doppler's insistence that Milo has been murdered; he panics as he searches the house for clues to a possible second murder; and finally he breaks down completely as the trapdoor of his own creation slams shut and ends his cossetted, comfortable life.

In many ways, the arc of Milo's story goes in completely the opposite direction. At first you possibly recognise and certainly sympathise with the man who did good against the odds, the man who has made something of himself through hard graft and sweat and doesn't deserve the ritual humiliation Andrew is meting out.

Yet if you scratch away at the surface, you soon find that there's more of Andrew in Milo's make up than he would like to admit. He's almost as self-centred and, despite his earlier tributes to his father's hard life and graft, you quickly realise he actually sees his father and his Italian heritage in general as something which will always hurt his social standing, something to keep locked away. Milo has done all he can to take on the persona of good English gentleman and enjoys the lifestyle that comes with it. He is just as much a snob as Andrew but won't admit it to himself.

Caine wasn't first choice for the role of Milo. Both Alan Bates and Albert Finney were considered, but it's difficult to see anyone else playing the role so well. I believe it's one of Caine's best performances - in some ways THE best - and he is more than a match for his illustrious co-star. After a number of cockney wide boy roles in *Alfie* and *The Italian Job*, he grabs the role of Milo by the scruff of the neck and never eases up for one moment. He reveals layer after layer of vulnerability, regret and terror, but ultimately a burning desire to no longer be the loser, to start being on the winning side.

Caine and Olivier got on well from the very start of filming, but in the early stages Caine was anxious at Olivier's inability to remember his lines. Olivier was well known for being able to recite hours of Shakespeare, but seemed unable to recall the simplest dialogue. Eventually, to the relief of all, he admitted he was suffering from nerves over his role in the National Theatre and had been taking Valium to help conquer the affliction. As soon he stopped taking the medication, his memory came back with such force that Caine suggested he start taking them again to even the playing field!

Caine admitted to being somewhat overawed by his co-star at the start of filming to the extent that he wasn't sure how he was supposed to address him. Over the course of filming, he gradually won Olivier's respect. In fact, after one particular scene, Olivier embraced him and announced: "When we started, I saw you as skilled assistant. I now see you as a partner."

The two performances on their own would have made *Sleuth* an incredibly watchable film anyway, but what takes it to the next level and adds the cherry on the top is the direction of Joseph L. Mankiewicz.

After such huge successes as *A Letter to Three Wives*, *All About Eve*, and *Suddenly, Last Summer* (as well as somehow managing to wrestle a coherent film out of the mess of *Cleopatra* - a film that nearly killed him), Mankiewicz' career had somewhat tailed off, but he's a perfect fit for *Sleuth*.

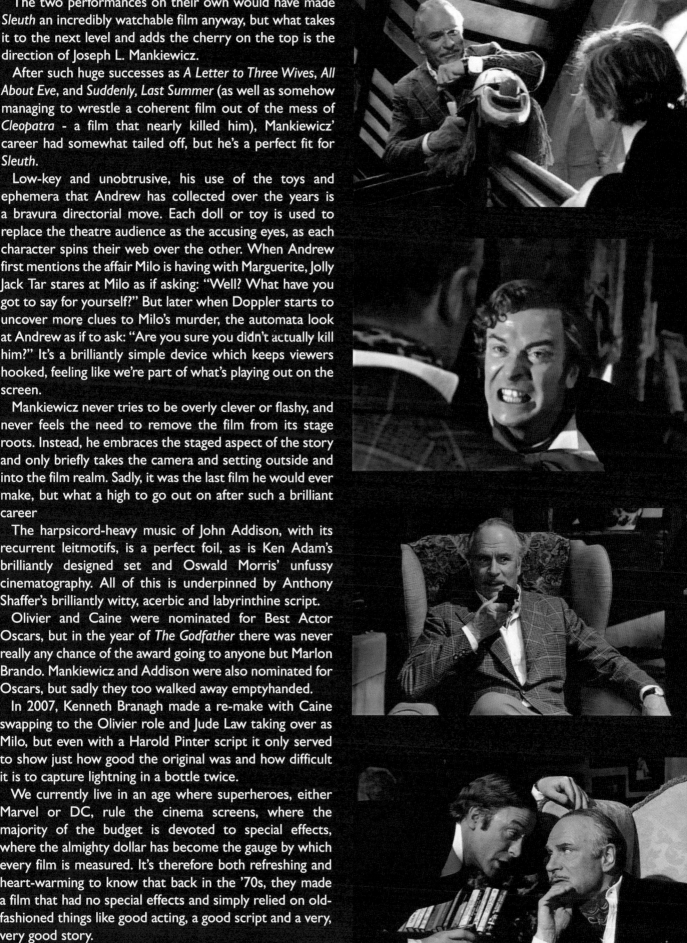

Low-key and unobtrusive, his use of the toys and ephemera that Andrew has collected over the years is a bravura directorial move. Each doll or toy is used to replace the theatre audience as the accusing eyes, as each character spins their web over the other. When Andrew first mentions the affair Milo is having with Marguerite, Jolly Jack Tar stares at Milo as if asking: "Well? What have you got to say for yourself?" But later when Doppler starts to uncover more clues to Milo's murder, the automata look at Andrew as if to ask: "Are you sure you didn't actually kill him?" It's a brilliantly simple device which keeps viewers hooked, feeling like we're part of what's playing out on the screen.

Mankiewicz never tries to be overly clever or flashy, and never feels the need to remove the film from its stage roots. Instead, he embraces the staged aspect of the story and only briefly takes the camera and setting outside and into the film realm. Sadly, it was the last film he would ever make, but what a high to go out on after such a brilliant career

The harpsicord-heavy music of John Addison, with its recurrent leitmotifs, is a perfect foil, as is Ken Adam's brilliantly designed set and Oswald Morris' unfussy cinematography. All of this is underpinned by Anthony Shaffer's brilliantly witty, acerbic and labyrinthine script.

Olivier and Caine were nominated for Best Actor Oscars, but in the year of *The Godfather* there was never really any chance of the award going to anyone but Marlon Brando. Mankiewicz and Addison were also nominated for Oscars, but sadly they too walked away emptyhanded.

In 2007, Kenneth Branagh made a re-make with Caine swapping to the Olivier role and Jude Law taking over as Milo, but even with a Harold Pinter script it only served to show just how good the original was and how difficult it is to capture lightning in a bottle twice.

We currently live in an age where superheroes, either Marvel or DC, rule the cinema screens, where the majority of the budget is devoted to special effects, where the almighty dollar has become the gauge by which every film is measured. It's therefore both refreshing and heart-warming to know that back in the '70s, they made a film that had no special effects and simply relied on old-fashioned things like good acting, a good script and a very, very good story.

Nicholas and Alexandra

The Fall of the Romanov Empire

by Julian Hobbs

Nicholas and Alexandra is a fascinating example of the expensive, serious-minded all-star historical epic that the UK and Hollywood just don't make any more, more's the pity. Combining the large scale and the intimate, the film is at its most affecting when focusing on the latter, particularly the relationship between the Tsar and Tsarina. That's how it should be, of course, given the movie's title… but there's another remarkable historical tragedy playing out here involving the fate of millions of their subjects, a tragedy almost impossible to do justice to in a feature film, even one with a three-hour-plus running time. Still, all the talented artisans involved deserve credit for bringing this important story to the attention of mainstream western audiences, who knew little of how the Russian Revolution came about despite it being one of the most seismic events of 20th century history. And, viewed as a purely visual spectacle, the Romanov court is brought sumptuously to life through the art direction of John Box and his team and the immaculate costuming of Yvonne Blake and Antonio Castillo. All received well-deserved Oscars for their work.

James Goldman and Edward Bond's literate screenplay wisely starts the action in the tumultuous year of 1905. Russia is defeated in a disastrous war with the Japanese over the Korean peninsula; hundreds of peaceful protesters are shot dead by guards as they attempt to march on the Imperial Palace to air their grievances to the Tsar (Michael Jayston); and the Tsarina (Janet Suzman) finally gives birth to a baby boy, the one male heir to the throne (the four daughters they already have don't get a look in). That one spark of good news soon turns potentially tragic when the baby, Alexis, is diagnosed with hemophilia and could die from an episode of internal bleeding at any time. With the finest doctors in the land unable to offer any help, Alexandra in desperation seeks the aid of the infamous mystic Rasputin (a star-making turn from Tom Baker), who does indeed seem to have some healing powers. Alexis recovers, seemingly miraculously, after the monk visits his bedside.

Of course, whatever one thinks about Rasputin's alleged healing powers, his drunken debauchery can be taken as a given. As he inveigles his way into the heart of the Russian monarchy, he beds many ladies of the aristocracy and scandalises the royal court in the process. This feeds into the disgruntlement of the common people who are already reeling from the horrors of war and the ensuing economic collapse. The propaganda machine goes into overdrive, and pamphlets are widely circulated which claim Rasputin is sleeping with the Tsarina. She can barely afford such scandal, being already deeply unpopular with the masses because of her German heritage and inability to deliver a (healthy) male heir to the throne.

In reality, the monarchists wanted Rasputin out the way as much as the revolutionaries wanted him around to cause further damage to the Romanov name. His infamous assassination - surely rife with cinematic possibilities - is the most misjudged episode in the film. Political correctness was not exactly the order of the day in 1971, and the aristocratic plotters are portrayed as obviously gay and unbelievably sadistic killers, giggling endlessly (and incredibly annoyingly) as they poison, shoot and brutally beat the monk with chains. Surprisingly, his subsequent dumping in an icy river and death from hypothermia is omitted entirely. (Hammer's more disreputable *Rasputin: The Mad Monk* (1965/6?) depicted the prolonged nastiness of the murder rather more wholeheartedly).

Away from the court is where the big story really plays out, and director Franklin J. Schaffner offers easily digestible chunks of history. There are snapshots depicting the grim life of Russian factory workers; we see future revolutionary leader Kerensky (John McEnery) demanding democratic change from the Duma floor (the Russian parliament, but little more than a talking shop); and the in-exile Lenin (Michael Bryant) and his rival Trotsky (a baby-faced Brian Cox) argue about strategy before eventually joining together to form the Bolshevik party.

For a movie obsessed with getting its historical details right, one might be surprised to discover the fact that Nicholas had assumed full command of Russia's military forces in 1915 isn't even mentioned in the film. This is especially remiss, since the Tsar's involvement in that disastrous war effort played a far bigger part in the fall of the Romanovs than the antics of Rasputin. If one wants to nitpick over historical accuracy, it's also worth noting that Stalin wasn't even in Moscow during the October Revolution (ironically, Stalin's own propaganda machine made him the real hero of the hour) and Prime Minister Stolypin's assassination actually happened two years earlier than depicted, in September 1911 to be precise. These are but small caveats to what is otherwise a meticulously researched and historically accurate work.

Like many big-name directors who emerged during the '60s and '70s, Schaffner had made his name through television, winning prestigious Emmy awards for his small-screen dramas. He was at his peak by 1971, following up the science fiction classic *Planet of the Apes* with *Patton: Lust for Glory* both of which scored big at the box-office and the Oscars. Truth be told, Schaffner is obviously more comfortable with the all-American bombast of General Patton than the incompetent leadership of the bloody-minded but essentially spineless Tsar Nicholas.

But the expert playing of Jayston (who looks uncannily like Nicholas) and Suzman (who beat first choice Vanessa Redgrave to the role) make us empathise with this deeply flawed couple, who, in the eyes of many, were responsible for millions of deaths.

Indeed, the tragedy is that Nicholas took the advice of Alexandra over more sensible, pragmatic politicians, advisers and military commanders: both believed in the divine right of monarchs. This is the drama's most convincing element, brought to life by nuanced playing from the leads, who aren't afraid to appear unsympathetic, even downright stupid at times. On the flipside, they obviously have a deep love for each other and are devoted to their five children. This keeps us engaged on an emotional level, particularly as the screws tighten in the final stages, where exile and imprisonment lead to indignities, humiliation and far worse.

Careful to balance things out, Schaffner has the Romanov naysayers express their views of 'Bloody Nicholas' and his disastrous rule. The most cutting comments are provided by the Tsar's captors, played by the likes of Ian Holm and John Wood. Funnily enough, their work carries more dramatic punch than that provided by big hitters Laurence Olivier, Anthony Quayle, Michael Redgrave, Jack Hawkins, Eric Porter and Harry Andrews. They are wheeled on and off to deliver authoritative, if shallow, cameos as various important dignitaries of the Romanov court, often just to

keep us up to date on the political action away from the Palace. Their roles in the drama echo their elder statesman position in British theatre and cinema. Nevertheless, this Who's Who of acting talent circa 1971 ensures a rewarding viewing experience for nostalgia buffs.

Equally arresting are the blink-and-you'll-miss-them appearances by up-and-coming talents like Brian Cox and Steven Berkoff, playing Bolshevik revolutionaries. Then there's Alexander Kerensky - the now-forgotten provisional Prime Minister who masterminded the February revolution. He is bought vividly to life by John McEnery, who captures perfectly his florid, melodramatic, undeniably rousing oratorial style.

However, the one real breakout performance comes from Tom Baker who was still a few years away from landing the *Doctor Who* gig and the

cultural immortality that went with it. Despite his famous booming theatrical voice, Baker dials it down here as the imposing monk. His scenes with Suzman are cannily played, showing him to be more an arch manipulator than a holy mystic, shrewdly exploiting the Tsarina's discomfort around strangers and fears for her son's health. His cinematic monk is certainly better groomed than the real Rasputin, who was known for rarely bathing and having filthy lank hair and dirty, talon-like fingernails. Even with these physical drawbacks he was a hit with the opposite sex, and Baker translates that hypnotic charisma with consummate skill.

Many would say the production, like Rasputin, could've done with a little more dirt under its fingernails, which was a criticism widely levelled by contemporary critics more

enamored of the spikier work coming from young auteur filmmakers like Bob Rafelson, Dennis Hopper, William Friedkin and other 'New Hollywood' directors who were making a splash in 1971. Respectable historical dramas were seen as an anachronism - younger audiences preferred more confrontational fare like *A Clockwork Orange, Five Easy Pieces, The French Connection* and so on. Schaffner's box-office hot streak well and truly ended with *Nicholas and Alexandra.*

Indeed, its financial failure, alongside that of David Lean's *Ryan's Daughter* the previous year, is often ascribed to the rise of the New Hollywood scene. Events in Tinseltown at that time had some parallels with the Russian Revolution (e.g. the new guard replacing the old), but large scale historical epics still had big appeal around Oscar season. *Nicholas and Alexandra* received six nominations, including one for the all-important Best Picture award. Perhaps rightly, it only picked up gongs in the technical categories. Even so, there's a strong case to be made for Suzman as Best Actress of the year, though she was pipped at the post by Jane Fonda for *Klute* (giving some indication of the clout the young upstarts had with the Oscar crowd). Despite being a respected mainstay of British theatre, Suzman was not a fashionable 'name' actor. It's interesting to note, too, that the equally good Jayston wasn't nominated at all.

Producer Sam Spiegel probably had half an eye on the prestigious awards season when *Nicholas and Alexandra* went into production. In 1962 he'd scored a major success with *Lawrence of Arabia,* but fell out with its director, the incomparable David Lean, during the production of *Doctor Zhivago,* three years later. Once could say this 1971 production was his riposte to the Lean film, telling another epic Russian tale with production values to match and all the British acting talent money could buy. Spiegel also

bought onboard such heavyweight Lean collaborators as Freddie Young and John Box, whose work is exemplary as ever and perhaps explains why this feels more like a David Lean picture than a Franklin J. Schaffner one.

Despite the huge scope, Columbia afforded Spiegel slightly less money than he'd been granted for his Lean-directed endeavors. There are no cutaways to the cinematic possibilities offered by the war on the Eastern Front, nor indeed even much of the events of the 1917 Revolution. But points are sometimes made, quite devastatingly, through smart editing: the 1905 massacre of peaceful protesters is carefully mounted but the violence is only shown briefly. Schaffner cuts away from the beginning of the melee to focus on the aftermath, with gallons of blood being hosed away from a stone mural of the Tsar. All the gratuitous violence in the world couldn't have made the point more forcibly.

The drama really starts to bite when Nicholas is forced to abdicate. From here, the family are exiled and put under house arrest, and moved three times to less and less salubrious quarters and increasingly unfriendly guards. After the often unfocused first half, the story is entirely theirs, sometimes to a claustrophobic degree;re there are no cutaways to an earnest Lenin and Trotsky discussing their possible fates (Lenin wanted a show trial for Nicholas until the escalating civil war led to more drastic measures). Schaffner nails the winding-down to inevitable tragedy more than capably, helped by the sensitivity of Jayston and Suzman, not forgetting Roderick Noble as Alexis, who, though gravely ill, displays the sort of fight that has completely left his broken father. If Nicholas always behaving in a dignified manner as the situation worsens says something about the UK/Hollywood tendency to portray royalty in an overly romantic fashion, it works for the downward spiral of the drama. That said, the way the Tsar breaks down in tears in front of his beloved following abdication is striking for the rawness of emotion on show. The princesses are also allowed to develop as more fully rounded characters in the latter stages, making for a sobering contrast to the giggly, carefree schoolgirls seen tormenting their long-suffering tutor in happier times.

Finally, the murder of the family along with their physician, Doctor Botkin (the ever-reliable Timothy West) is not graphically presented but has real impact, thanks to simple staging and understated playing. The family are made to assemble in a small room on the pretext of being moved to another house. The focus, for a few minutes, is simply on them and their agonizing wait, with no dialogue or score to deflate the tension. When the killers assemble, the realization of what is happening hits Alexis and he quickly kisses his father on the cheek before the firing starts. It's a sobering and powerful denouement which stays with you after the credits have rolled and allows us to forgive

some of this prestige picture's undoubted flaws. On a purely personal note, it made me contemplate how many similarly horrific acts would befall Russian families over the next three decades, through a brutal civil war, famine, Stalin's Great Terror and the near-apocalyptic struggle of the Second World War.

THE DEEP

by Dawn Dabell

"There is no terror greater than the
unknown and no place more unknown than
the world under the sea."
Robert Shaw

Peter Benchley penned a number of bestselling novels which prominently featured themes of a nautical nature, from killer sea creatures to bloodthirsty pirates. Unquestionably, his most famous piece was his first work of fiction 'Jaws', which, following its hardback release in 1974, remained on the bestseller list for a whopping 44 weeks. As a result of its success, 'Jaws' was adapted for the big screen in 1975, with Benchley teaming up with screenwriter Carl Gottlieb to co-write the screenplay and Steven Spielberg at the helm. Universal decided to take a risk with *Jaws* by releasing it during a traditionally quite time for cinema - the bleak summer period. Due to a large marketing campaign, this decision paid off when the film opened with a strong weekend box office return of $7 million (a record at that point). This summertime success was to change the face of cinema from that point forth, with *Jaws* becoming the forerunner of the 'summer blockbuster'. The notion of summer blockbusters was further cemented in 1977 when George Lucas released *Star Wars*.

Fuelled by the success of his first work of fiction, Benchley hoped to replicate his winning formula. It was after visiting the wreck of the cargo vessel *Constellation*, which had sunk north-west of Bermuda, that Benchley came up with the

premise for his latest novel. Some reports suggest the *Constellation* sank after hitting the Western Blue Cut reef, but other sources cite that it was possible that the ship had in fact hit the bow of the sunken steamer *Montana* located nearby (the wreck of another steamer is also located within close proximity to both vessels, the *Lartington*). The *Constellation* was carrying an assortment of cargo which included medical supplies - iodine, penicillin, insulin, adrenaline and morphine - and it was these sunken supplies in their ornate glass vials which inspired Benchley's second sea-based novel 'The Deep' (1976). Instead of a man-eating shark terrorising the locals of a seaside town, this time the focus was moved to treasure hunting in the depths of the ocean. For those hoping for another bloodthirsty sea creature, Benchley threw one into the mix albeit as a 'supporting' monster.

Young couple David Sanders (Nick Nolte) and Gail Berke (Jacqueline Bissett) are vacationing in Bermuda. They go scuba diving and come across the sunken vessel *Goliath*, a WWII ammunition ship. They find a number of artifacts including a coin, a spoon with *Golitah* carved on it, and an ampoule of liquid. The couple's discovery comes to the attention of Henri Cloche Bondurant (Lou Gossett Jr), the leader of a drug gang on the island who is interested f the contents of the glass ampoule. Wanting to learn more about the artifacts they discovered while diving, Sanders and Berke seek the help and advice of Romer Treece (Robert Shaw), a lighthouse keeper who has some experience of treasure hunting. With Treece's help, they discover that the coin is actually a Spanish medallion from a wreck located directly beneath the *Goliath*. The trio carry out research on the medallion and come across a list of treasures which may have been on the sunken ship. Cloche is desperate to get his hands on the thousands of ampoules full of morphine located on the wrecked *Goliath*. Treece plans to help the young divers with their treasure hunt but is forced to strike a deal with the drug kingpin to keep him and his henchmen at bay while they carry out their dives. With Cloche stopping at nothing in his attempts to get his hands on the morphine, will the young couple get their hands on their treasure? To add another level of danger to the dive, they need to avoid the clutches of a large and aggressive Moray eel which has taken up residence inside the wreck (the 'supporting' monster I was talking about earlier).

Although *The Deep* didn't gross as much as *Jaws* at the box office, it did beat the record set for its opening weekend, taking $8.1 million (Columbia's best opening box-office up to that point) compared with $7 million for Universal's *Jaws*. Audiences probably wanted to see if the makers would manage to top the heights and scares of *Jaws*, so rushed out to see this follow-up Benchley adaptation on the opening weekend. Another factor for the increase in bums on seats could be that *The Deep* features one of the most iconic images from 70s cinema. Mention this film in passing conversation, or on any one of many film-themed groups on social media, and you can guarantee the discussion will quickly move from the film itself to the merits of Jacqueline

Bisset and her notorious white wet T-shirt. Controversially, an image of Bissett scuba diving while wearing the said white T-shirt was widely used despite the fact she had refused to give her consent. It is thought that David Doubilet, a photographer from the 'National Geographic' who was present in some of the underwater sequences, may have taken the photograph (though this has never been confirmed). The picture created a lot of publicity for *The Deep*, especially when it turned up in ad campaigns in publications like 'Playboy' and 'Penthouse' without Bisset's approval. Producer Peter Guber once quipped: "that T-shirt made me a rich man!" Over the years, Bisset has stated that she hadn't realised her top had become so see-through under the water. In an interview, she said: "I thought, okay, well, we're underwater. Big deal. You won't see anything underwater!" She was extremely dismayed when the production company decided to use these images for a lot of the marketing and promotional materials. She went on to state: "I felt betrayed because it's all people talked about and it had nothing to do with the work we put into the film." In more recent years, she revealed that she "tried to get the thing stopped; I tried to get an injunction on them" (a move which proved unsuccessful). One thing which can't be denied though, is that it was a brilliant piece of marketing. Heck, it's still being discussed more than 40 years on!

As so much of the action takes place in the ocean, both cast and crew had to learn how to dive before shooting could commence. Guber, Nolte, Bissett, Shaw and Gossett Jr et al, had never dived beforehand. The training was a very gruelling experience. As director, Yates was required to dive whenever his cast took to the depths. He'd had prior experience of diving while working on *Murphy's Law* (1971) but struggled with the equipment and didn't find it

enjoyable due to terrible earaches. Working with the instructors here, he overcame his issues and became a more accomplished diver. Looking back, it must have been quite an achievement to get so many of the inexperienced or first-time divers among the cast and crew to shoot so much underwater footage. Of the main supporting cast, only Eli Wallach's scenes were shot entirely above the water, so presumably there was no requirement for him to join in with the diving lessons. Discussing the strains of underwater filming, Nolte stated at the time: "I've been down in the water four or five times every day for the last three months and I've reached the point where the physical strain has become too much for me. It takes a long time for a human being to acclimatize to an environment as unnatural to him as the water but I may soon be growing gills."

The open water diving sequences were filmed near Peter Island in the British Virgin Islands. For the exteriors of the wreck, the *RMS Rhone* was used. *Rhone* was a UK Royal Mail ship which was shipwrecked just off the island during a hurricane in the late 1800s. Unfortunately, the *Rhone* didn't have any interior left where scenes featuring its hull could be filmed, so an alternative interior had to be created. Filming was moved to Bermuda, where a purpose-built structure was created to function as an underwater sound studio. This man-made structure was 120 feet long and 30 feet deep and contained an estimated 1 million gallons of fresh seawater and thousands of fish. Columbia Pictures proudly described it as the largest underwater set ever constructed. The structure featured a number of areas, including a replica of the *Rhone* (standing in for the

Goliath), the interior of the Spanish galleon and the lair of the bloodthirsty Moray eel.

In an early cut, a prologue was shot featuring the *Goliath*'s shipwreck sequence during the war. Although it didn't make it into the final edit, the sequence (which features familiar B-movie actor Cameron Mitchell) can be viewed on the 101 Films Blu-ray release in the extra features.

The underwater scenes are a visual treat. In other features set partly or wholly in the depths of the ocean, these sequences can appear dark and it can be tricky to follow the action. In *The Deep*, there is a real clarity in the photography, with bright and fully discernible underwater footage of the actors and marine life. This is down to the director of cinematography Christopher Challis learning how to dive, meaning he was able to spend a lot of time in the water alongside the director and the cast. Challis was nominated for a BAFTA Award for Best Cinematography, but lost out to cinematographer Geoffrey Unsworth for his work on *A Bridge Too Far*. This wasn't the only nomination *The Deep* received. It was also nominated for an Academy Award for Best Sound and a Golden Globe for Best Original Song.

Although *The Deep* is often cited as Nolte's motion picture debut, he had already appeared in *Return to Macon County* alongside Don Johnson in 1975. *The Deep* however thrust Nolte into the cinematic limelight and led to him becoming a sought-after Hollywood actor. His on-screen chemistry with Bissett is highly believable, plus he is athletic enough be convincing in his fight sequences with the Cloche's henchmen. Bissett, who had previously worked with Yates as the female lead in *Bullitt* (1968), was the ideal choice for the part of Gail.

Not only does she look the part visually - breathtaking whether kitted out in her scuba gear or an evening dress - she also puts in one of her best on-screen performances. She may be fondly remembered by many for those wet T-shirt scenes, but she really looks the part in the dramatic moments or when gliding through the ocean alongside the sea-life.

Having starred as the shark-hunter Quint in *Jaws*, Shaw seemed the perfect choice for the role of Treece in yet another Benchley adaptation. As one would expect, he plays the part wonderfully and brings real colour and toughness to it. Although not the main character, he does receive top billing on most theatrical posters, with Bissett billed second. As a relative newcomer, Nolte (who might also have been in the running for top billing) is generally placed third in the pecking order. Sadly, Shaw died of a heart-attack in 1978 at the age of 51 while shooting *Avalanche Express*. Given the proximity of his tragic death to the release of *The Deep*, it's quite an achievement that he managed to carry out the demanding diving scenes himself.

Vincent Canby of 'The New York Times' wasn't very taken with *The Deep*, feeling that: "The story, as well as Peter Yates's direction of it, is juvenile without being in any attractive way innocent, but the underwater sequences are nice enough, alternately beautiful and chilling." One aspect which most critics agreed on was the visually appealing underwater filming. Whether you agree with Canby about the rest of the on-screen action, it's certainly worth setting aside time to view *The Deep* for these sequences alone. Despite the big opening weekend, some viewers came away a little disappointed at the time, having gone in expecting another thrilling underwater horror film only to be greeted with a lengthy, plotty and mainly horror-less adventure flick. Over the years, people have warmed to it and it is now a fairly well-regarded and oft-seen movie which continues to be screened on TV, re-issued on various home media formats, and enthusiastically discussed by fans of '70s cinema.

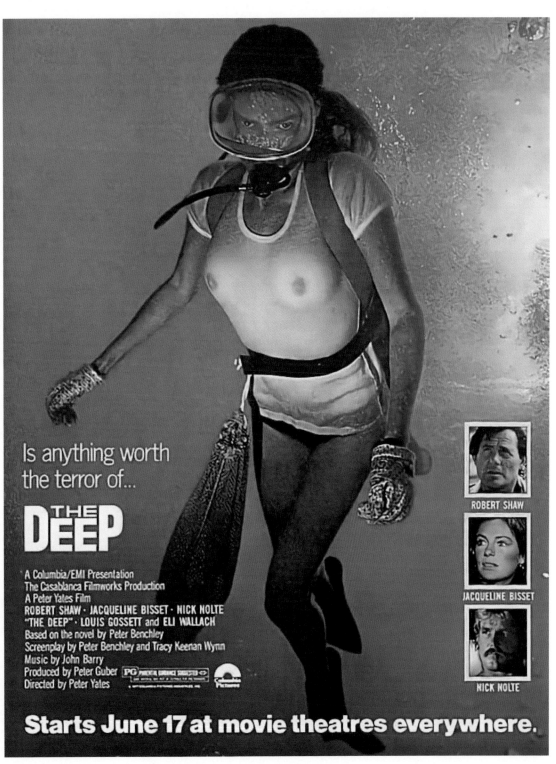

Is anything worth the terror of...

THE DEEP

A Columbia/EMI Presentation
The Casablanca Filmworks Production
A Peter Yates Film
ROBERT SHAW · JACQUELINE BISSET · NICK NOLTE
"THE DEEP" · LOUIS GOSSETT and ELI WALLACH
Based on the novel by Peter Benchley
Screenplay by Peter Benchley and Tracy Keenan Wynn
Music by John Barry
Produced by Peter Guber PG
Directed by Peter Yates

ROBERT SHAW

JACQUELINE BISSET

NICK NOLTE

Starts June 17 at movie theatres everywhere.

GOING APE IN THE 1970S

by John Harrison

"WHERE MAN ONCE STOOD SUPREME... NOW RULE THE APES!"

Though it had its beginnings in the previous decade, the *Planet of the Apes* saga became very much a phenomenon of the early '70s. Directed by Franklin J. Schaffner and based on a 1963 novel by French author Pierre Boulle, *Planet of the Apes* (1968) hit American screens around the same time as Stanley Kubrick's *2001: A Space Odyssey* (1968). While *2001* was beautifully abstract and cerebral, *Planet of the Apes* rooted itself more firmly in the action-adventure genre, with Rod Serling's screenplay giving it just the right amount of social satire, not to mention one of cinema's most startling and memorable final moments.

The success of both *2001* and *Planet of the Apes*, commercially and critically, proved that science-fiction was a viable subject to be explored beyond the confines of

low-budget popcorn cinema and presented as respectable, prestige studio productions. While fans of *2001* had to wait over fifteen years for a cinematic follow-up, in Peter Hyam's rather underrated *2010: The Year We Make Contact* (1984), Arthur P. Jacobs, the producer of *Planet of the Apes*, recognized immediate potential in a sequel, as did the studio behind the movie, 20th Century Fox. And the revolutionary prosthetic apes make-up, designed by Oscar-winner John Chambers, was simply too good to confine to just one movie. As a result, the *Apes* characters and continuing adventures became familiar to movie and television audiences during the first half of the '70s.

For anyone not at all familiar with the original film, *Planet of the Apes* starred Charlton Heston as Colonel George

Taylor, a 20th Century astronaut whose space vehicle is flung into a time-warp, crashing on a barren, unknown planet some two-thousand years in the future. Though life exists on this planet, the evolutionary process is the reverse of what had occurred on Earth. In this strange place, simians are the dominant master race, possessing speech, intelligence and religion, while humans are the mute, lower form of race, hunted by the bloodthirsty gorillas and hated by most apes for carrying disease and destroying their crops. Finding solidarity with a humane chimpanzee couple, archaeologist Cornelius (Roddy McDowall) and his medical doctor wife Zira (Kim Hunter), Taylor defies the warning from Dr. Zaius (Maurice Evans) and heads out on horseback into the desolate wastelands known only to the apes as The Forbidden Zone. Riding along the rocky shoreline with his beautiful but mute companion, Nova (Linda Harrison), Taylor comes across the rusting, ruined remains of the Statue of Liberty, half buried by the sands of time. Falling to his knees in shock and disbelief, Taylor realises that this strange planet he has crash-landed on is, in fact, his own home, Earth, hundreds of years after being ravaged by some distant, devastating atomic holocaust.

Interest in a sequel to *Planet of the Apes* began taking shape not long after it debuted to strong box-office and positive reviews, and *Beneath the Planet of the Apes* went into production in early 1969. Though the film was completed and ready to go by late 1969, Fox waited until April of 1970 to release it, as the studio wanted to ensure they had a commercial hit during that financial year, to help offset some expensive duds they had produced in the late '60s. So while *Beneath* is technically a film produced in the '60s, it was the first of the *Apes* movies to debut in the '70s, and it does actually evoke a nice balance of both decades, with moments reflecting what had happened in the later part of the '60s (in particular, the debates about war and the young chimpanzee protesters), while other aspects were more indicative of what was to come the following decade (the mutant humans giving off the

disturbing vibe of some early '70s UFO cult that have been gripped by *Chariots of the Gods?* fever). With a big job to do, and a heavy reputation to live up to, *Beneath* provided the perfect transition for further entries.

Directed by Ted Post from a screenplay by Paul Dehn, who had written the Bond classic *Goldfinger* (1964), *Beneath* broadens the *Apes* landscape to include the subterranean, atomic-charred ruins of New York City, where a race of mutated humans, who have developed telepathic powers during their centuries underground, worship a 20th Century doomsday bomb, and fear its use will be the only defence against the onslaught of an approaching ape army. While the brutish General Ursus (James Gregory) leads his gorillas into battle (his infamous motto being: "The only good human… is a dead human!"), Taylor meets up with Brent (James Franciscus), another astronaut who has crash-landed while following Taylor's trajectory, and the pair launch a desperate, last-ditch attempt to save the Earth from annihilation.

With its nihilistic ending, *Beneath the Planet of the Apes* would have to rank as one of the bleakest science-fiction films ever produced. The cataclysmic climax was apparently instigated at the request of Charlton Heston himself, who only agreed to reprise his role of Taylor as a favour to Richard D. Zanuck, then president of 20th Century Fox. Zanuck required the participation of Heston in order to guarantee financing for the film. Heston reluctantly agreed to come back, but only for limited amount of time, and only if they agreed to kill his character off once and for all. Screenwriter Dehn, who was brought into the fold after treatments by Pierre Boulle and Rod Serling were rejected, went one better and decided to kill off the entire planet. After all, the Statue of Liberty ending from the first film had such a dramatic impact that it was already becoming a part of science-fiction cinema folklore. The expectation (and pressure) was there to end the sequel on an equally dramatic and memorable note. Heston was all too happy to be the one to push the button, figuring the end of the world would virtually guarantee the end

of the series, and any further obligation he may have to it. While director Post hated the ending as it provided no glimmer of hope for humanity, he went along with it at the insistence of Zanuck, who was angry at being forced out of the studio by his formidable father as punishment for commercial failures like *Doctor Doolittle* (1967).

Though not quite in the same class as its predecessor, *Beneath the Planet of the Apes* is still, at its core, a very solid and entertaining science-fiction action-adventure film. If *Planet of the Apes* is the big Friday night premiere movie, then *Beneath* is its perfect Saturday afternoon matinee follow-up. Unfortunately, *Beneath*'s allocated five-million-dollar budget was slashed in half at the eleventh hour, thanks to the Julie Andrews musical *Star!* (1968) bombing hard at the box-office. The reduction in budget does get reflected in the rather flat, almost made-for-television look which *Beneath* often exudes, as well as in the make-up department, with many of the background apes shuffling around in obvious masks, rather than prosthetics. The primary ape make-up, however, is just as impressive as ever, and almost topped by the incredible job done to bring the mutant humans to life, their outer layers of flesh burned away to reveal a nightmarish collage of veins, muscle sinew and brain tissue.

The plot of *Beneath* is also rather thin and very light on characterization, but it more than compensates for this with its grand concepts and some exciting action passages, staged with an assured hand by Post, a director who would soon tackle another sequel in *Magnum Force* (1973), the follow-up to *Dirty Harry* (1971). Tanned and muscular, James Franciscus makes a solid action hero, even if his character seems thrown in as a convenient Heston/Taylor clone, since Heston's actual screentime in the movie amounts to less than twenty minute. Roddy McDowall was unavailable to reprise his role of Cornelius in *Beneath*, so David Watson was brought in with little fanfare and the hope that most people wouldn't notice (though the film does start off with a reprise sequence from the first film, so technically McDowall is still in the film). Linda Harrison, Maurice Evans and Kim Hunter all return to help bring a strong sense of continuity, and in the fearsome Ursus, James Gregory gives us the enduring face of simian aggression (a pity his character was never to return). As the pretty female mutant Albina, Natalie Trundy, actress wife of Arthur P. Jacobs, makes the first of her appearances in an *Apes* film. She would return for the remaining three sequels, playing both human and simian characters.

Having destroyed the world, it would seem there was nowhere left to takes the *Apes* franchise, but the impressive box-office for *Beneath* amply demonstrated that audiences were hungry for more adventures. Paul Dehn was brought back to pen another sequel, and he came up with an ingenious idea that would not only provide a logical way to continue the story, but would also freshen up the tone, and start a clever loop that would take us through the evolutionary history of the apes over the remaining three films. Next to producer Arthur P. Jacobs, Dehn would become the figure most responsible for the direction in which the *Apes* story arc went.

Dehn's idea for the third film supposes that, as the climactic events of *Beneath* were taking place, Cornelius and Zira, along with another chimpanzee scientist, Dr. Milo, manage to retrieve the wreckage of Taylor's spaceship from the bottom of the lake in The Forbidden Zone, and somehow get it operational. The ship reaches orbit just as the Earth explodes, the resultant shockwave sending the vehicle, and its three ape-onauts, hurtling back through time, eventually landing in 1973 in the Pacific Ocean off the Californian coast. Initially treated by the world with curious bemusement, attitudes turn more worrying and sinister once the authorities learn about the eventual fate of Earth and the human race, and the fact that Zira has become pregnant.

Released in May of 1971, *Escape from the Planet of the Apes* was the first of the films to be a true product of the '70s, and it certainly reflects it, though perhaps more from a stylistic point of view than a thematic one. Aesthetically, the fact that the events of the story take place in 1973 means the film reflects a very early '70s feel in terms of fashions, vehicles, hairstyles and architecture. And while it still has its serious subtexts, along with a very sombre and tragic conclusion, *Escape from the Planet of the Apes* is overall a lot lighter in tone than the previous two films, with many of the early moments depicting Zira and Cornelius adapting to 20th Century city life played with a classic "fish out of water" comedic edge. The film is also much more intimate and character-driven than the first two entries, and has a climax that is more personal - and personally tragic - than the apocalyptic revelations that ended both *Planet* and *Beneath*.

Escape certainly has its fans, many of whom rate it as their favourite entry in the series, though for myself it took a few viewings to really begin to appreciate it. As a kid watching it on TV, I thought it was too much of a shift from the primitive landscapes of the first two films, which for me were a big part of the appeal of the whole *Apes* concept. Repeated viewings, however, have helped endear it to me on a much stronger level. It's the most human story in the series, and works so well in no small part because of the wonderful performances by McDowall and Hunter, who hold it together and take the prime focus as the only two simian stars (save for Sal Mineo, who plays Dr. Milo in the opening scenes, before his character is killed by an agitated zoo gorilla). Bradford Dillman and Natalie Trundy also make for an appealing human couple, playing doctors in animal psychology who befriend Cornelius and Zira, and ultimately aid them in their

73

attempt to escape the clutches of Dr. Otto Hasslein (Eric Braeden), a physicist who wants the two talking chimps and their newborn to be terminated in order to protect the survival of the human race. Also aiding the protection of the three primates is Armando, a circus owner and ape lover. Played by veteran Mexican star Ricardo Montalbán, the confident, charming, loyal and flamboyant Armando is one of the more memorable human characters to feature in the *Apes* series.

While *Escape* only made about 60% of the US box-office earned by *Beneath*, it was still more than popular enough to warrant further entries, especially when taking into account the huge worldwide appeal which the films enjoyed, and the lower budget which *Escape* was produced on, thanks to location shooting and the reduced need for multiple ape make-ups. The *Apes* films were becoming what the studios like to call "base hits": movies that aren't expected to break box-office records, but have a big enough built-in audience to guarantee some sort of profit. They were safe bets in a very unpredictable business.

For the inevitable next film, things took a decidedly darker and more violent tone, in stark contrast to *Escape*'s family-oriented adventure. Directed by J. Lee Thompson, with a screenplay once again penned by Paul Dehn, *Conquest of the Planet of the Apes* (1972) stands as the *Apes* film which is most overtly reflective of the early '70s. Set in the North America of 1991, the movie paints a bleak, cold portrait of a totalitarian state, where apes - trained initially as pets to replace the dogs and cats that had been eradicated by a space virus - are now abused as slaves. The now-adult and intelligent, talking son of Cornelius and Zira, soon to be self-named as Caesar (McDowall), arrives for the first time in a big city with his keeper Armando (Montalbán again), under the guise of being a performing circus ape. Naturally, Caesar is horrified to see the way in which his fellow apes are treated by humans, and he begins to instil a rebellious spirit into his fellow primates, hoarding weapons in secret until the gathering ape army launches a fiery assault on the city, overthrowing the government and its brutal, cold-hearted ruler, Governor Breck (a wonderful performance by Don Murray).

Effectively ending with the birth of the Planet of the Apes, *Conquest* always alternates with *Beneath* as my own personal favourite of all the *Apes* sequels. *Beneath* was the first *Apes* film I ever saw (a 16mm print projected onto the wall at our grade school), while *Conquest* was the first I got to experience in a theatre (at the very '70s-futurstic Astrojet Cinema and Space Centre, situated next to Melbourne's Tullamarine Airport and sadly long gone). But even apart from the nostalgic memories attached to both films, I just love the tone and vibes that each carries and the individual stories and messages they put across. While *Beneath* fed on our fears of global warfare and nuclear holocaust, *Conquest* focused on the social upheaval that

was going on, right then and there, on the streets of America. The parallels in Dehn's screenplay to American slavery, revolution, and the Black Panther movement may be as subtle as a sledgehammer, but they are powerful nonetheless, and they work. There is a stark brutality to *Conquest* that is unique to the series, and if *Live and Let Die* (1973) is considered the 'Blaxploitation Bond', then *Conquest of the Planet of the Apes* would have to bear a similar distinction for its own saga.

Though the city in which the events of *Conquest* take place in is not specified, a lot of it was shot on location in Century City in Los Angeles. Once a backlot owned by Fox before being sold-off in the early '60s, it was by

1972 a sea of modern architecture, high-rise businesses and shopping plazas. With its severe, angular architecture and mostly bland grey and chrome colour scheme, broken only by the green and red of the apes' jumpsuits and the odd patch of grass, it provides a very suitable landscape for the film's apocalyptic events to unfold in.

Saddled with the lowest production budget for an *Apes* film to date (a mere US $1.7 million), director Thompson does an admirable job of giving the film some scope. As in *Beneath*, inferior masks can clearly be spotted on many of the background apes, but visually Thompson gives the film an interesting look, utilizing some lovely matte paintings to expand the horizons of the city, and by dressing the police and other authoritarian figures in all-black, very Nazi-esque uniforms. Even the citizens of this America dress in very drab, muted colours, which add to the oppressive, downbeat atmosphere that the film quite brilliantly generates.

Conquest also indelibly connected Roddy McDowall as the face of the *Apes* franchise, and its most recognizable name. While McDowall was an integral part of an impressive ensemble cast in the first movie, and an equal half of a potent duo in *Escape*, in *Conquest* the weight of the entire film pretty much falls on his shoulders. And certainly, he does not disappoint, delivering what is his best performance from behind the make-up. McDowall's Caesar is required to run through a gamut of emotions throughout *Conquest*, from innocence and bewilderment to disillusionment and heartbreak, to anger and violence. Particularly impressive is the scene where Caesar discovers that Armando has killed himself on order to avoid police interrogation. The motion, sadness and rage which McDowall generates from under all that prosthetic make-up is quite palpable.

Sadly, when *Conquest of the Planet of the Apes* was test-screened, some audiences reacted negatively to its moments of graphic violence (the film features some

very gory shots of facial gunshot hits to both humans and apes) and its downbeat ending. It was important to their commercial success at the time that the *Apes* films appealed to a wide family audience, with a G-rating preferred (both *Beneath* and *Escape* had been rated G in the US, despite some rather bloody moments in the former). As a result, Fox not only cut out all of the blood, they brought McDowall back into the studio to record a new speech, dubbing it in and re-editing the footage to try, not very successfully, to match the original words. In the new speech, rather than incite the apes to continue their shedding of human blood, Caesar implores them to put down their weapons. Now they have overpowered the humans, they can afford to be humane and dominate them with compassion. For years, the original cut of *Conquest* was impossible to see, but thankfully it has become available as a bonus feature on recent Blu-ray editions. It is absolutely the more impactful and superior of the two versions, even if the original ending does somewhat contradict the direction the story takes in the next adventure.

J. Lee Thompson returned for what would be the final of the original series of *Apes* films, *Battle for the Planet of the Apes* (1973). However, perhaps stung by the criticism that greeted *Conquest* and its more violent overtones, Thompson played it very safe indeed in *Battle*, delivering a mostly kiddie-friendly action-adventure film which ends the series on a disappointing fizzle rather than a memorable bang. There's no doubt the budget, as with *Conquest* a mere US $1.7 million, prevented *Battle* from achieving the grand scope you would expect to end such an epic saga. The climactic titular battle sees the Caesar-led apes, along with their human companions whom they mostly now live peacefully with, facing off against the race of underground mutant humans. Unfortunately, the showdown has none of the scale it deserves, and certainly doesn't deliver what was promised on the film's poster: "The most suspenseful showdown ever filmed as two civilizations battle for the right to inherit what's left of the earth!"

In fact, the epic battle involves no more than a couple of dozen people, and a few treehouses and old military jeeps being blown up in the middle of a forest. The budget allotted to *Battle* was so restrictive that Thompson made sure to film every explosion and big stunt shot from several different angles and lengths, so they could be used in editing to create the illusion of a more grand scale. Even with this technique, the action sequences barely rise above that of a Saturday morning live-action kids TV show. Perhaps the most interesting thing about *Battle for the Planet of the Apes* is the eclectic range of names recruited to play some of the new ape characters, including Claude

Akins as gorilla leader Aldo, singer/ entertainer Paul Williams as Virgil (an orangutan advisor to Caesar), and John Huston as The Lawgiver, who narrates the story from the distant future to an integrated audience of young apes and humans.

Finishing with a close-up on a statue of Caesar as a tear rolls down from one of its stone eyes, *Battle for the Planet of the Apes* may have signalled the end for the original run of films, but it was merely the start of the *Apes* marketing blitz. A repackaging of all five *Apes* movies, screened as marathons at drive-ins and hardtops under the banner 'Go Ape!', proved immensely popular, as did the television premieres of the first three movies. It led to a flood of merchandise hitting the shelves between 1974-1976, including Mego action figures, model kits, board games, masks, bubble gum cards, a Marvel comic book magazine, jigsaw puzzles, trash cans, narrated adventure story record LPs, and so much more. For a while there, if you could slap a picture of an ape on it, then chances were someone would buy it, no matter how ludicrous the product seemed (a *Planet of the Apes* wading pool, anybody?). Convinced there was still more mileage in the property, Fox ordered a live-action television series to be put into production, which debuted on CBS on September 13, 1974.

Once again starring Roddy McDowall, this time playing the chimp Galen (pretty much a variation on Cornelius), the *Planet of the Apes* TV series also featured James Naughton and Ron Harper as Burke and Virdon, the latest human astronauts to find themselves stranded on the ape-dominated Earth of the far future. Unlike in the first two movies, the humans in the TV series weren't mute or primitive. The humans were also allowed to live relatively free, in their own villages and society, though the threat of trouble and violence from the apes, particularly the gorillas,

remains ever present. These changes to the human-ape dynamic were clearly made to allow more variety and drama into the teleplays, and to provide some lines for the actors who guest starred in human roles each week (a roster that includes names like William Smith, Robert Conrad, Sondra Locke, Jackie Earl Haley and Marc Singer). While Burke seems accepting of the situation he has found himself in, Virdon is driven by a desperate hope that a small

computer disc, which he retrieved from their crashed spacecraft, may hold the key to their eventual return to their own time and families.

Few of the television episodes were particularly memorable or revelatory, with each week seeing a slight variation on the same theme: Virdon, Burke and Galen narrowly escape the clutches of the brutish gorilla General, Urko (Mark Lenard), usually hiding out in a remote village or ruined city building until the danger has passed.

The highlight episode for me has always been *The Trap*, in which an earthquake traps Burke and Urko in a ruined San Francisco subway train tunnel, and Burke has to convince the human-hating gorilla that they must work together in order to survive. To create further tension, Burke also has to try to prevent Urko from setting eyes on a faded poster hanging on the subway walls, advertising the local zoo with a picture of a gorilla in a cage, being gawked at by a bunch of humans.

Ultimately, the only real thing that the *Planet of the Apes* series had going for it was the lingering appeal of the concept and make-up, and of course the charisma and charm of Roddy McDowall. Beyond that, there was little to recommend about it, or distinguish it from so many other formulaic shows of the period, though it certainly still serves its purpose as light entertainment, and Lenard's Urko, modelled clearly on James Gregory's Ursus from *Beneath*, deserves his place in the pantheon of memorable Apes characters. And Lalo Schifrin's title theme is terrific, exciting and original while still clearly evocative of Jerry Goldsmith's scores for the early films. But, in a sign that perhaps the concept was finally running its course with the general public, ratings for the television series were modest at best, and it was cancelled after just one season and fourteen episodes. In 1980, ten episodes of the series were edited into five ninety-minute TV movies, which were sent out as a package with titles like *Back to the Planet of the Apes, Forgotten City of the Planet of the Apes* and *Farewell to the Planet of the Apes*. Usually broadcast in an afternoon timeslot, McDowall filmed new introductions for these faux telemovies, in full make-up as an older Galen, though sadly these have not been included on any home video release thus far, and may well be lost.

In terms of film and television productions, the last hurrah for the *Apes* saga in the '70s was *Return to the Planet of the Apes*, an animated series which originally ran on the NBC network in the thirty-minute timeslot on Saturday mornings. Produced by the famous DePatie-Freleng company, *Return to the Planet of the Apes* was certainly an interesting venture, more creative and experimental than the live-action series. While the apes in the animated show were visually similar to what fans of the saga had become used to (though for some reason, Urko is given a bright orange tunic and helmet), their society was more highly advanced, more in line with Pierre Boulle's original novel.

Naturally, the animated format allowed for *Return to the Planet of the Apes* to depict concepts that would have been unworkable or too expensive in live-action. So apart from the apes driving cars, jeeps and armoured vehicles, the animated series also gave us sea serpents, giant apes, monster birds and even an ape flying a vintage World War II era fighter plane! Interestingly, the continuing storyline which ran throughout the animated series incorporated several characters from across the *Apes* universe. There is Cornelius, Zira and Zaius from the early films, though instead of Ursus, we are given Urko from the TV series

as the leader of the gorilla army. Nova is also included, as is Brent, but original astronaut Taylor is never mentioned. And in this story arc, the Brent character knew Nova when she was still just a little girl, before he lost contact with her and her tribe in a sandstorm. The telepathic, underground city-dwellers from *Beneath* also feature prominently in the series, and interestingly mistake Judy, the lone female astronaut, for a long-promised god, thanks to an old NASA tribute bust of her which they have had in their possession.

While Roddy McDowall had no participation in *Return to the Planet of the Apes*, some continuity with the films was still established by the casting of Austin Stoker, who provides the voice of astronaut Jeff Allen. Stoker had previously appeared as MacDonald in *Battle for the Planet of the Apes*, playing the brother of the character which Hari Rhodes played in *Conquest*. Like the live-action series, *Return to the Planet of the Apes* lasted just one season, with thirteen episodes aired between September and November of 1975. It effectively marked the end of the original *Apes* era, although Marvel continued to publish its *Planet of the Apes* comic magazine until February of 1977, coming to an end with its twenty-ninth issue. Ballantine

also published a trio of paperbacks in 1976 that were based on *Return to the Planet of the Apes*, though the covers featured stills from the movies and live-action series rather than the animated show. Published under the pseudonym of William Arrow, the first and third of these paperbacks were written by the great William (Bill) Rostler, who was not only a noted science-fiction author but also spent time as a sexploitation filmmaker, directing the classics *Agony of Love* (1966) and *Mantis in Lace* (1968), the latter something of a psychedelia-drenched exploitation masterpiece.

Any lingering awareness which the general public had for *Planet of the Apes* was washed away by the galactic tsunami which occurred in the wake of the release of *Star Wars* in May of 1977. Suddenly, sci-fi cinema had a whole new, exciting face, and a parade of memorable characters to go with it. It's likely that Fox's experience with the *Apes* phenomena held them in good stead when planning and dealing with the sudden demand for *Star Wars* merchandise. While Chewbacca may have been sci-fi's hairiest cinematic hero of the late '70s, for the previous ten years that honour belonged well and truly to the roster of incredible *Planet of the Apes* characters that kept fans of the series going bananas with excitement.

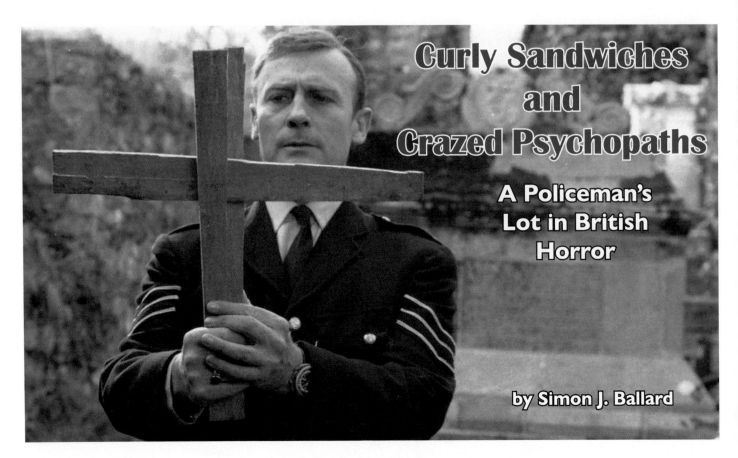

Curly Sandwiches and Crazed Psychopaths

A Policeman's Lot in British Horror

by Simon J. Ballard

In times gone by, when wayward vampires and rampaging monsters were on the loose, you would send for the militia or a good ol' torch-wielding mob to charge around with no clue what was going on. However, as Britain entered the 1970s and bloodsucking killers were on the attack, or famous horror actors disappeared, or people entered the London Underground and never came back, who were you gonna call? Why, the ever dependable, indefatigable, dogged Police Force, of course!

The present-day netherworld of the Universal cycle of horrors featured marvellous police officers like Lionel Atwill's Inspector Krogh in *Son of Frankenstein* (1939). But for this piece, I'm going to concentrate specifically on the British Police Force, mostly the Criminal Investigation Department (CID), and the way they're depicted in several contemporary horror films from the '70s. The selection is a personal one and, in discussing the various officers and their cases, spoilers will be inevitable. After all, these files are open to inspection... not locked away under the Official Secrets Act!

Detective Superintendent Bellaver (Alfred Marks) in Scream and Scream Again.

Let's open our notebooks and take down in evidence a film that marked something of a departure in style for Amicus Productions. Moreover, a film which made much of the triple-distilled horror of Vincent Price, Christopher Lee and Peter Cushing appearing in one picture... well, sort of. Although made in 1969, *Scream and Scream Again* is included here by the skin of its teeth thanks to a more brutal, cynical style of storytelling that would become the norm as the decade progressed. And because it was released on the 1st January, 1970.

Ostensibly the tale of scientist Dr. Browning (Price) and his experiments to replace humankind with specially created replicas, *Scream and Scream Again* takes in a fascistic fictional East European state, a jogger who suffers a heart attack as soon as the credits are done, and the hunt for a killer who leaves his victims drained of blood.

SCREAM AND SCREAM AGAIN

The latter plot strand is where my focus lies. The man in charge of the investigation is Detective Superintendent Bellaver (Alfred Marks). Initial impressions of him are that he's a man you'd love to watch at work though you wouldn't want to be on the receiving end of his waspish, acerbic tongue. Impatient, irritable and justly rude to a press photographer at the scene of the crime, it's immediately apparent he's a man under pressure.

Turning up at Browing's grand house, Bellaver's opinion of the rather obtuse valet/butler is that he's a "snotty little bastard." He makes this remark to his colleague Jimmy Joyce (Clifford Earl), and it tells us much about Bellaver - that he dislikes pomp and ceremony; that he comes from a honest-to-goodness working class background; that he hates those who think themselves above him. Over-used phrases like 'no nonsense' and 'doesn't suffer fools gladly' were never more apt than they are regarding Bellaver. When Dr. Sorel (Christopher Matthews) presents him with an audio recording of the post-mortem findings of a female victim, Bellaver is irritated at such fancy, modern methods - a nice, succinct report on paper will do just fine, thank you very much. And who can blame his world-weary attitude when there is a demented killer on the loose and the station sandwiches are "curling up like Chaplin's boots"?

Marks is a delight to watch. An actor and comedian who began his career in variety, he is just the man to play the biting yet hilarious Bellaver. Each acid remark is perfectly timed, and his commanding presence cuts a swathe through all he purveys. He is bombastic, never still, but fully calm and in control with a healthy dose of cynicism as mayhem billows around him during the hunt for the killer.

Michael Gothard plays the tormented but compelling killer Keith, a broodingly handsome man who is later revealed to be more than the sum of his parts. His initial introduction throws us unto a seedy world not unlike that featured in *Peeping Tom* (1960). He targets innocent young women and - in one of Amicus' more harrowing moments - assaults a lady in a darkened, grubby alley, clawing at her face and strangling her. This is a far cry from the sensual vampiric seductions of Hammer's *Dracula*.

Police and pursuer come dangerously close as PC Sylvia Griffin (Judy Huxtable) sets herself up as a honey trap for Keith, much to the consternation of her husband, DC Griffin (played with great nervous effect by Julian Holloway). Interrupting the culprit as he attempts to gorge on the blood from Sylvia's wrist, the police manage to drag her to safety. An exhilarating

car chase ensues (a full four-and-a-half minutes long), anticipating many a set piece in the TV show *The Sweeney* later in the decade. This is before Keith abandons his nifty little sports car and heads on foot towards a quarry - the quarry in a quarry trying to shake off his quarry (I'll stop saying quarry now). Keith demonstrates superhuman strength as he runs, leaps and scales a sheer edge, not to mention - when finally caught - utilising a famously drastic means of escape after being cuffed to a car bumper. The pursuit lasts a quarter of an hour before Keith finally takes his acid trip (or, rather, trips into a vat of acid). The look of total bewilderment on Bellaver's face as the vat bubbles and dissolves the suspect sums up this rather bizarre case. With only a torn hand with unusual synthetic properties left to examine, Bellaver instructs Sorel to keep it safe. "If it's as unusual as you say it is, it might get up and walk away, mightn't it?" he quips. A hilarious line, delivered deadpan by Marks, which references *Dr. Terror's House of Horrors* (1965) - you can't beat that!

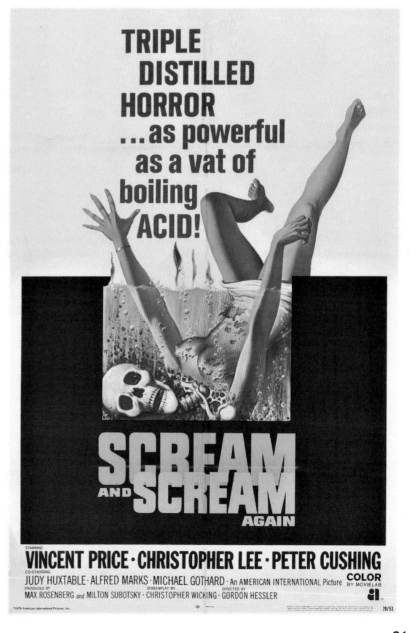

Impotent anger flares for Bellaver when the case is closed and Browning is declared off limits, with more than a whiff of corruption in the air. The beleaguered Bellaver's own personal file is closed permanently when Konratz (Marshall Jones) - who has featured majorly in Browning's experiments - gives him a terminal cold shoulder. It's rather distressing to see such a wonderful character cut dead, blood dribbling from his mouth. Now I know what it must have been like for audiences experiencing the demise of Jack Warner in *The Blue Lamp* back in 1950!

Inspector Holloway (John Bennett) in The House That Dripped Blood.

For Inspector Holloway (John Bennett), the case surrounding actor Paul Henderson (Jon Pertwee) seems superficially rather more prosaic than a blood-sucking murderer, though it is couched within its own air of mystery. After renting an imposing, secluded house from a property agent named A.J. Stoker & Co., Henderson went missing. Scotland Yard's Holloway is sent to investigate and soon imposes himself on the local constabulary. He isn't the least bit shy about expressing his attitude toward them.

The House That Dripped Blood (1971) gives us John Bennett as Holloway. Bennett was a theatrical actor who had trod the boards for the Royal Shakespeare Company and the Royal National Theatre and would also make a name for himself on television, including two villainous turns in *Doctor Who* with Jon Pertwee and Tom Baker. He would appear in films up to and beyond *Minority Report* (2002).

Holloway's investigation into Henderson forms the framing device for Amicus' third portmanteau film. Whilst not on screen for any great length, his presence is nevertheless the pivot around which the tales take place. Local Sgt. Martin (John Malcolm) hands him a file on the tenants who had rented the house previously and whose stays were not exactly pleasant. Holloway is disdain personified, and Bennett gives a cold, hard and withering performance. Martin admits the case is not in his line at all. "Your report makes that very clear," Holloway icily retorts. He opens the file and begins to read about 'young' couple Charles and Alice Hillyer (Denholm Elliott, Joanna Dunham) who came to the house so that he could write his next horror book about a strangler named Dominick. The file ends with Charles dead and a madman standing over his wife's body claiming to be Dominick. Holloway sinks his head into his hands and accepts a mug of tea with ill grace while the sergeant claims the house itself somehow had a hand in the deaths. The inspector is in no mood for such fantasies.

With tie undone and cigarette on the go, the crossed furrows of Holloway's face show no sign of abating as he moves on to read the file on retired stockbroker Philip Grayson (Peter Cushing). A visit to the letting agent Stoker (John Bryans) yields yet more nonsense as far as Holloway is concerned. Stoker explains how he tried to warn the potential tenants about the house and its secret. Tantalisingly, when enquiring about the Inspector's own home - a flat, it turns out - Stoker comments: "Bit on the cold side?" before shrugging off further explanation. It's a neat little exchange, feeding us clues about the house and its effect on people, not to mention the personality of Holloway himself.

When told by Stoker that the next tenant, John Reid (Christopher Lee), was supposedly killed by his young daughter using voodoo, Stoker explains it was not the girl or the belief in black magic that killed Reid, but the house. Such superstition is not for this hard-nosed copper. All Holloway wishes to know about is Paul Henderson, so he decides it's time to visit the house and the framing device becomes part of the fourth segment. In the climactic scenes, the experienced, fact-seeking Scotland Yard policeman comes face to face with Henderson, now undead baring vampiric teeth. It's interesting that for a man with both feet firmly planted in everyday reality, he instinctively knows that a stake through the heart is needed as he thrusts a broken stool leg into Henderson. That's not the end of it though, as he hadn't reckoned on the presence of Henderson's girlfriend Carla (Ingrid Pitt)…

Bennett's performance keeps things grounded, especially during the climax, which is perhaps needed when Pertwee is gurning for his country. Director Peter Duffell's original intention was to shoot the finale as a sped-up b&w silent homage, which might have been at odds with Bennett's grounded performance.

Chief Inspector Oxford (Alec McCowen) in Frenzy.

One can imagine the bachelor Holloway from *The House That Dripped Blood* sitting in his flat enjoying TV dinners and convenience foods. This would seem a haven of edible delight for Chief Inspector Timothy Oxford (Alec McCowen) whose wife has taken a course in the Continental School of Gourmet Cooking whilst he investigates 'The Neck-Tie Murderer' in Alfred Hitchcock's *Frenzy* (1972). We catch him enjoying a full English breakfast in his office at Scotland Yard as though to line his stomach in preparation for what horrors may await at home.

Oxford and his unnamed wife (Vivien Merchant) add a dash of humour to a particularly grim yet satisfying dish of psychopathy in Hitchcock's thriller. Barry Foster's sex maniac Robert Rusk is the man Oxford must catch, though it takes a while for him to realise it. As he sits at the dinner table discussing the case with his wife, Oxford

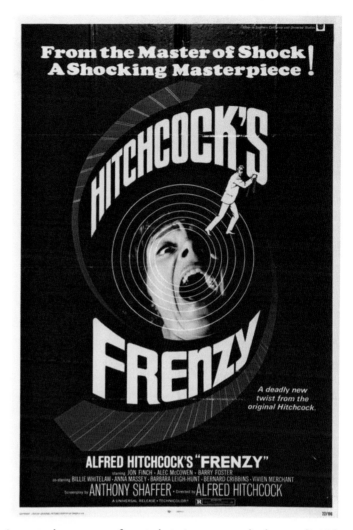

is served a starter of *soup de poisson*, a murky brown liquid wherein dwells such 'delights' as conger eel and frogfish. This is followed by *caille aux raisins* (quail with grapes to you and me). We are privy to his thoughts on suspect Richard Blaney (Jon Finch) as he attempts to wrestle a tiny morsel of meat from the tiny, scraggly bird, his wife cheerily oblivious to his obvious discomfort.

McCowen started out in theatre in 1950, joining the RSC in 1962. He would portray a kindly vicar who isn't really a vicar in Hammer's *The Witches* (1966) as well as being cast as Q in the unofficial James Bond film *Never Say Never Again* (1983). In *Frenzy*, Oxford is a kind, gentle copper, as exemplified when he questions eyewitness Monica Barling (Jean Marsh). He is also an excellent judge of character. When Blaney is found guilty and swears vengeance on Rusk while being led away from the dock, most policemen may have left matters. Certainly, all the evidence points towards Blaney, hence his conviction. Yet Oxford decides to probe further, and of course his instincts prove entirely correct - instincts he shares with his wife's intuition over another course of culinary catastrophe as he is presented with *pied de porc a la mode de caens* - a pig's foot, basically! McCowen's comic timing is perfect as he coughs out the mouthful of trotter while his wife's back is turned and the doorbell rings.

Inspector Murray (Michael Coles) in Dracula A.D. 1972 and The Satanic Rites of Dracula.

Food is no doubt far from the mind and stomach of Inspector Murray (Michael Coles) as he gazes upon the mutilated body of Laura Bellows (Caroline Munro), despite the cold, rational stare as he is informed by the pathologist the body was drained entirely of blood. It's *Dracula A.D. 1972* (1972), and although we are under no illusions as to the culprit, Murray has some rather interesting speculations of his own. He refers to the possibility of it being a cult murder, similar to those experienced in America not so long ago, an intriguing conjecture from one who seems otherwise a normal, run-of-the-mill Scotland Yard detective. But there is more

The Count is back, with an eye for London's hotpants... and a taste for everything.

to Murray than simple, methodical policing. Coles is the standout star of the film after Christopher Lee and Peter Cushing. Indeed, his scenes with Cushing as Lorrimer Van Helsing are some of the best in the movie and show what an imaginative and intuitive police officer Murray is. He is also mad for executive toys!

Rather neatly, Van Helsing's potential knowledge (and the fact his granddaughter Jessica was friends with Laura) are reason enough for Murray to pay him a visit. The mention of the draining of blood strikes a chord. "Are there such people, who get their kicks this way?" the Inspector asks. London is a very cosmopolitan city, after all! His reaction to the notion the killer may be a vampire says everything about the man. At first, he looks to his sergeant, as though to confirm he did hear right, then he instinctively dismisses the idea with a nervous smirk. Van Helsing proposes: "You dismiss the possibility?" Murray pauses, ponders and replies: "Dunno." He is deadly serious when he assures Van Helsing he does not think him a crackpot. It makes him a fulsome character, not a one-dimensional cypher blustering on about how such things are ridiculous. When he sniggers a little as Van Helsing discusses his grandfather's fate, it's obvious he is doing so because he is scared a whole new world of terrifying possibility has just been opened to him.

From Van Helsing's esoteric, booklined study to Murray's own rather modern office at Scotland Yard, the Inspector still struggles to come to terms with the thought that vampirism is abroad. He may not ignore it entirely, but he has a tough time accepting it in the 'here-and-now' of twentieth century London. It's as if he can only accept vampires are real by thinking of them as belonging to another time and place. It is only at the sight of Johnny Alucard (Christopher Neame) fizzing like a bath bomb in his own tub that Murray comes face to face with an actual vampire, but by that point he has totally bought into their existence.

By the time of *The Satanic Rites of Dracula* (1973), Murray has been promoted to Special Branch. Or perhaps side-lined out of the way? After all, with all those unsolved

murders behind him, he may not have been a welcome presence at the Yard. Whatever would he have put in the case files?!

Nevertheless, his secret services are required by SI7 in connection with some pretty weird things going on at Pelham House, home to the resurrected Count Dracula (Christopher Lee). Naturally he brings Van Helsing (Cushing) and Jessica (Joanna Lumley) into the picture, the three of them acting like they're in a pilot for a spin-off series we'd love to watch. Special Branch officers are highly secretive, usually dealing in matters of political threat and terrorism of which Dracula's scheme is the most apocalyptic form of suicide killing.

Coles is on fine form again and engages in a rather fine double act with William Franklyn as an agent named Torrence. As they descend towards the cellar of Pelham House, indecision and nerves kick in once they face the door. "Well, you are the law," Torrence says, stepping back. There is also a nice, almost romantic chemistry with Lumley, replacing Stephanie Beacham as Jessica, and we can imagine love blossoming once she recovers from the hypnotic grip of the Count.

Inspector Calhoun (Donald Pleasence) in Death Line aka Raw Meat.

The only love experienced by Inspector Calhoun (Donald Pleasence) is to piss off as many people as possible. All in the line of duty, of course. Investigating the disappearance of James Manfred OBE (James Cossins), a big shit - sorry, big *shot* - in the city, Calhoun unwittingly discovers the results of a cave-in during Victorian excavations for the proposed Museum Underground Tube Station. The Man (Hugh Armstrong) is the last survivor and descendant of those left to die in the accident, a grunting cannibal who can only utter the meaningless words: "Mind the doors."

Gary Sherman's *Death Line* (1972) is perhaps the most viscerally gory of all British '70s horror movies, with a

long, lingering tracking shot of The Man's charnel house that stays in the mind for a long time. Light relief is gratifyingly provided by Pleasence as one of the most memorable of all policemen from '70s horror cinema. He would either have gotten on well with Bellaver from *Scream and Scream Again* or they would have clashed like alley cats, for they have much in common. The same jaded cynicism is present, as is the hatred for authority which is exemplified in his clash with MI5 operative Stratton-Villiers (Christopher Lee, in a cameo he took just to share a scene with Pleasence).

Before this, we see Calhoun, accompanied by Detective Sergeant Rogers (Norman Rossington), belligerently prowling around Manfred's opulent apartment. Helping himself to monkey nuts and whiskey whilst breaking into a drawer, Calhoun sneers with contempt and class hurt at the amount of money displayed before him. "Not a bad drum," he begrudgingly concedes upon entering.

Stratton-Villiers annoys him immediately. Tension is to the fore as the shadowy secret service agent meets the working-class copper. Told to walk away from the Manfred case, Calhoun visibly mouths the words "Fuck you." Meanwhile, the agent offhandedly waves away the Inspector, saying: "Why don't you go back to planting pot on people?" Lee and Pleasence are electrifying together.

BENEATH MODERN LONDON buried alive in its plague-ridden tunnels lives a tribe of once humans. Neither men nor women, they are less than animals.....they are the raw meat of the human race!

"Raw Meat" starring
Donald Pleasence · Norman Rossington · David Ladd · Sharon Gurney and Christopher Lee
screenplay by Ceri Jones based on an idea by Gary Sherman Technicolor ® produced by Paul Maslansky directed by Gary Sherman an American International release

Well, sort of. Due to the vast difference in height between them, Sherman only allowed the actors to be in the same shot once Lee was sitting down!

As far as his attitude towards students is concerned, Calhoun is equally contemptuous. Interviewing American student Alex Campbell (David Ladd), who found Manfred's prone form lying on the steps of Russell Square Tube Station, the Inspector does not disguise his disdain. He accuses Campbell of theft when he reveals he and girlfriend Patricia (Sharon Gurney) looked through Manfred's wallet in order to check if he was diabetic. And when he finds out the student is studying Economics, he sneeringly asks if Britain will profit from the Common Market. The exchange ends with Calhoun accusingly suggesting Campbell will join a protest march, before 'ordering' him to get a haircut, laughing happily to himself.

The interview is totally unprofessional, and utterly hilarious, which also describes the scene where Calhoun and Rogers get pissed in the pub, staying well beyond closing time. By all accounts, the scene was improvised, and it is just perfect as far as on-screen depictions of drunken behaviour are concerned!

When Patricia is kidnapped by The Man, Calhoun and various officers stumble upon the scene of degradation down below. The Inspector allows himself a heartfelt moment of pity when regarding the charnel house of rotting bodies. "What a way to live," he sighs. Perhaps more so than most, here is a horror film where the investigating officer is as much the focus as the terrors he faces. It works as a snapshot of Britain in the early '70s, as well as the public perception of the Police Force at the time, a perception that's not particularly flattering!

Chief Inspector Hesseltine (Robert Hardy) in Psychomania.

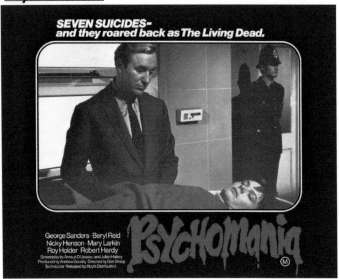

Whereas DI Calhoun was at the very core of *Death Line*, the police presence in biker horror *Psychomania* (1973) feels as though it's there merely because it's expected, not

necessarily to add to the story. Mind you, some rather exciting chase sequences under director Don Sharp are not to be sniffed at.

Investigating death and carnage in the wake of biker Tom Latham (Nicky Henson) returning from the dead is Chief Inspector Hesseltine, played by the ever fruity Robert Hardy. Sporting a Northern accent in this Home Counties-set feature, Hardy's Hesseltine investigates terror attacks perpetrated by members of the appropriately named Living Dead biker gang with a permanent pout edged on his face. One can sympathise with the Inspector as he flails about in the dark, for this is a case like no other, with dead bikers breaking their pals out of jail and impossibly bending bars in the process. This is way more serious than routine hooliganism perpetrated at the Hepworth Way Shopping Centre!

With the odds against him, Hesseltine plans to lure the Living Dead to a hospital morgue. Tom's girlfriend Abby (Mary Larkin) is still in the land of the living, so the copper plans to use her 'dead' body as bait. With Abby on the slab, Hesseltine and two uniformed officers stand guard. The camera tracks around the morgue slowly until eventually we see all three officers now lying dead in three chest freezers! A rather ignoble end for the Chief Inspector, though his loss is not as keenly felt as that of lovable grump Bellaver in *Scream and Scream Again*.

Inspector Boot (Milo O'Shea) in Theatre of Blood.

Nothing so supernatural plagues Inspector Boot (Milo O'Shea) of the Yard, merely the disgruntled murderous spree of a critically spurned actor. A simple case - if you

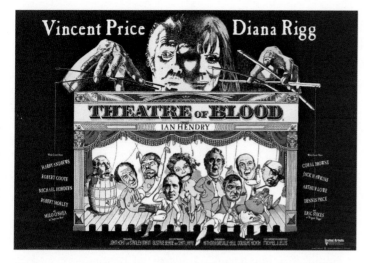

know your Shakespeare, that is! Played by Irish actor Milo O'Shea, Boot may have been twenty years in the force but nothing has prepared him to deal with death by spear-before-being-dragged-along-by-a-horse, a decapitation, or the removal of one's heart. All these methods of murder feature in the comedy of terrors *Theatre of Blood* (1973). And they don't end there. Almost all the critics who savaged Edward Lionheart (Vincent Price), Shakespearian actor par excellence, meet with deaths that will be familiar to students of 'Julius Caeser', 'Troilus and Cressida' and 'Richard III', among others.

Boot is initially hampered in his investigations because Lionheart, the leading suspect, killed himself after being humiliated by the assembled critics at an awards ceremony. We can also understand the copper's confusion when the head of Horace Sprout (Arthur Lowe) ends up on top of fellow critic Peregrine Devlin's (Ian Hendry) pint of milk. Horace is the third victim, prompting Boot to say to Devlin in a 'remarkable' expression of insight: "There's no doubt about it now. He's after you all!"

O'Shea is an amenable, likable presence for what is, in all honesty, a rather bumbling part, That said, the character befits a horror film which has distinct comedic aspects, however dark they may be. Boot is happy to accept Devlin's hypothesis that Lionheart is alive, and brings him aboard as their man with the knowledge of the Bard. They are also nicely aided by Sergeant Dogge (Eric Sykes). As performed by Sykes, there are one or two lovely touches, such as when Boot orders the subordinate to remove Sprout's head from the milk bottle. Tentatively producing a handkerchief, Dogge proceeds to blow his nose before ordering a constable to do the macabre job for him.

Despite offering police protection, seven of the critics end up viciously slaughtered, with one arrested after being goaded into murdering his wife. At times Boot seems nothing more than a passive bystander to Lionheart's extraordinary and deadly living theatre performance. A worried Devlin says: "There are only three of us left… surely the entire might of the London police force can stop us being killed." And he's right to be alarmed, because the

police officers are not exactly on the ball. The constable protecting critic Chloe Moon (Coral Browne) while she sits in a chair having her hair done only realises she has been electrocuted when smoke rises from her head in dense clouds.

They attempt to track Lionheart through his daughter Edwina (Diana Rigg), using a homing device. Dogge hides in the boot of Devlin's car on surveillance, but things end rather badly. With the complicit Edwina driving Devlin's car, Dogge reports via radio that the car has stopped, and he can hear a train approaching… his final words. Following the fiery demise of Lionheart and the trail of corpses left in his wake, I suspect Boot was given the, er, boot from the force and offered early retirement!

Sergeant Howie (Edward Woodward) in The Wicker Man.

A pension plan is not something Sergeant Howie (Edward Woodward) would be able to enjoy following the events of *The Wicker Man* (1973). Howie is a devout Christian sent to Summerisle in the Hebrides to investigate the disappearance of youngster Rowan Morrison (Geraldine Cowper). He is unaware he is setting foot into a trap designed to ensnare him as the perfect sacrifice to the islanders' Pagan gods in return for a healthier crop the following year.

Although the people of Summerisle, and their beliefs under Lord Summerisle (Christopher Lee), are seen as an affront to Christian dogma (and prove particularly offensive to Howie), the officious and overly pious nature of the sergeant makes the islanders seem more enlightened than him! We feel more sympathy toward *their* ways, *their* open honesty in matters of sexuality and youth, than we feel toward the repressed virgin copper sent among them. Woodward offers many moments of humanity which save the character and allow us to feel utter horror and despair at his ultimate fate. Despite the more cynical nature horror was taking as the '70s wore on, it's still genuinely shocking when we realise he isn't going to be saved at the last minute.

Although the UK theatrical print butchered the film and removed a whole night from the narrative, I must admit I prefer the way Howie's character is introduced in the heavily cut version. We see him landing at Summerisle but we have no pre-conceived ideas about his nature. This is fitting, as his religious leaning versus that of the islanders is revealed during the course of events. In the Director's Cut, we are privy to his churchgoing, his virginal engagement and his lack of humour, which prejudges him against us rather too soon. Peeling away the layers should run concurrently with the totally contrasting Lord Summerisle and his people - that way, we'd gain more intrigue and character interest.

Howie's outrage at children being taught the facts of life in no uncertain terms and witnessing young people dancing naked through fire are met with charming retorts from his lordship that not only sound acceptable, but preferable to the ways of the mainland. The meeting with Lord Summerisle is less a police interview, more a theological debate. "We're a deeply religious people," Summerisle tells the shocked Howie. To show that he disagrees, the sergeant points out the ruined church, the lack of priests, the "children dancing naked." Summerisle's counter argument, that it would be much too dangerous to jump through fire with clothes on, is a priceless rejoinder.

When Willow (Britt Ekland) provocatively sings her song, naked in her room in The Green Man inn adjacent to Howie's, he bubbles over with sexual desire and battles devoutly to suppress the temptation. I'm sure many of us find ourselves urging him on - go on, lad, go and enjoy a moment of humanity among the heathens!

Howie's righteous indignation certainly comes before his duties as a policeman. His opinions and moral outrage go far beyond his professional brief. The Director's Cut certainly makes it clear he is something of a joke on his own home turf, and one wonders, if he had survived the encounter with the Wicker Man, how likely his chances of advancement would have been.

Police officers often used to say: "If you can't take a joke, you shouldn't have joined." With '70s Britain proving such a hotbed of supernatural and earthly-bound terrors in these movies, a sense of humour would certainly be one of the main requirements to any officer of the law. That, and an open mind!

There was more to British crime in the '70s than blags, burglaries and wages snatches. Get your shroud on, you're nicked!

by Jonathon Dabell

If everything had gone to plan, *Hooper* would have been released early in 1976 under the title *The Stuntman* with Lamont Johnson directing and Burt Reynolds as leading man. Things were held up when producer-director Richard Rush filed arbitration proceedings against Warners because he was in the process of preparing a movie of his own called *The Stunt Man*. After lengthy deliberation, the MPAA ruled that Rush had a valid claim on that title and instructed Warners to come up with a different name for their movie. The arbitration proceedings dragged on for so long that by the time a decision was reached both Johnson and Reynolds had moved on to other projects. Thus, *The Stuntman* was shelved for the foreseeable future.

By autumn 1977, Reynolds had enjoyed an unexpected box office smash with *Smokey and the Bandit* for stuntman-turned-director Hal Needham. He had also started a high-profile relationship with his co-star from that film, Sally Field, and had reunited with her for his soon-to-be-released, self-directed black comedy *The End*. Smelling an opportunity to ride the crest of *Smokey*'s success, Warner Bros. announced plans to revive *The Stuntman*. Reynolds and Field would star, and Needham would be at the helm. The new title would be *Hollywood Stuntman*, though Richard Rush - whose own project was still in development (it didn't see light of day until 1980) - remained unhappy and contemplated taking Warners to arbitration proceedings again unless they were willing to change it voluntarily. Several weeks into their shooting schedule, Warners and Needham finally settled on a new name for their film, calling it *Hooper* in reference to the eponymous 'hero' Sonny Hooper, played by Reynolds. Needham had been an uncredited stunt performer as

far back as the mid '50s and had risen through the ranks to become the highest paid stuntman in the business. He reportedly fractured 56 bones, twice broke his back, punctured a lung and knocked out many of his teeth during his long and dangerous career. *Smokey and the Bandit* marked his directorial debut and came second only to *Star Wars* at the American box office in 1977. He was very much in demand despite being an inexperienced director. His background in stunt work made him the perfect choice to take over from Lamont Johnson when *Hooper* finally went into production. It was an added bonus that he had already worked with Reynolds and Field. The project was ideal for Reynolds too, since he had done some uncredited stunt work early in his career, as well as a number of falls and driving sequences in his action pictures. In many cases, the studios and producers were unaware he was performing these risky sequences, neither granting permission nor putting in place sufficient insurance for him to be doing them. In fact, an unauthorised 'burn' stunt in 1972's *Fuzz* had nearly gone tragically wrong, and the actor was fortunate to walk away with nothing more than minor injuries.

"Stunt men have the most exciting job in the movies. I wanted to do *Hooper* because it was about stunt men," the actor explained. You can sense what a happy time Burt and everyone else had while working on the movie. The cast and crew convey a tangible sense of 'family' - real chemistry, camaraderie and togetherness which almost oozes from the screen. Charles Schreger of the 'Weekly Variety' noticed it too, writing: "It's been too long since actors projected as much on-screen chemistry as Burt Reynolds, Jan-Michael Vincent, Sally Field and Brian

Keith do in *Hooper*. Individually, the performances in this story of three generations of Hollywood stuntmen are a delight. And Hal Needham's direction and stunt staging are wonderfully crafted. But it's the ensemble work of this quartet, with an able assist from Robert Klein, which boosts an otherwise pedestrian story with lots of crashes and daredevil antics into a touching and likable piece."

Hooper got surprisingly good reviews all round considering that it spends much of its running time depicting crashes, smashes, trips, falls and leaps performed by beer-guzzlin', fun-lovin', yahoo-hollerin' stunt performers. Hard-to-please critics like Jane Maslin of the 'New York Times', Richard Corliss of 'New Times', David Denby of 'New York Magazine' and Kathleen Carroll of the 'Daily News' all wrote favourably about it. Lou Gaul went so far as to claim that: "Burt gives his most attractive performance yet in the role of an ace stuntman." Daniel Ruth of the 'Tampa Tribune' went further still, hailing director Ashby as: "the Michelangelo of mayhem, the Fellini of falls, the Sartre of stunts."

It's a straightforward story, at least on the surface. Middle-aged stuntman Sonny Hooper (Reynolds) is beginning to feel the stress and strain of his profession. Years of daredevil stunts have left him with a busted body. Medication helps to a point but, according to the doctor, he's one bad fall from being paralysed for good. While working on an action pic titled *The Spy Who Laughed at Danger*, Sonny continually clashes with the arrogant director Roger Deal (Robert Klein) who is something of an egomaniac and has little regard for the safety of his stuntmen. Sonny's girlfriend Gwen (Field) is worried for Sonny, and her fears are only perpetuated by the fact that her father Jocko (Keith) was himself the best in the business in his day but now suffers various health complaints due to years of bumps,

bruises and broken bones.

There is also a new, young hotshot on the scene who might just take Sonny's mantle as the greatest stuntman of them all. Ski (Jan-Michael Vincent) is a big fan of Sonny's work but wants to take things to the next level. He too ends up working on *The Spy Who Laughed at Danger*, further threatening Sonny's status as the top dog in his field. Roger the director decides to change the film's ending to include an incredible earthquake sequence in which the hero will drive a car through a town while chimneys fall, buildings collapse, vehicles crash and things explode. The big finale will involve a bridge collapsing into a gorge, leaving a 325-foot chasm which the hero must rappel across. But Ski comes up with a more ambitious suggestion: why not leap over the gorge in a rocket-powered car? This draws a nervous gasp from everyone in the room as the existing record for a rocket-car jump is only 187 feet. Roger is desperate to have the jump in his movie, and Sonny - despite the obvious danger, Gwen's protests, and the enormous risk to his already-damaged body - knows he will have to be Ski's co-pilot if the stunt is to be performed successfully.

Hooper offers more than mere stunts and mayhem, especially in the way it depicts an old-timer wanting to achieve one final amazing feat before time takes it beyond his reach. There are many movies from the late '60s and the '70s which show an aging, battered hero performing one last heroic act, perhaps to prove his masculinity, perhaps to save a friend or perhaps simply to 'go out in style'. Sam Peckinpah in particular had made this a major theme in his work and, while *Hooper* is too light in tone and style to be compared with Peckinpah's examinations of world-weary masculinity, the similarities are there nonetheless. (Curiously enough, Bloody Sam was working on a light, crash-'n'-smash-themed movie of his own at the time - the

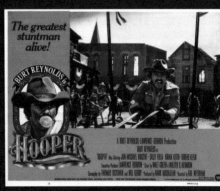
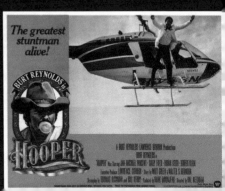

Another way in which *Hooper* offers something more is in its gallery of colourful characters. So many of them stick in the mind - Reynolds' exuberant hero, Field's sweet but worried girlfriend, Vincent's dauntless rival, Keith's grizzled and likable old pro, Klein's maniacal, bullying director (reportedly modelled on Peter Bogdanovich). Even the 'smaller' characters are memorable and amusing, like Tony (Alfie Wise), the director's perpetually ass-kissing assistant; Max (John Marley), an old-school producer who shows genuine affection and admiration for Sonny; and Cully (James Best), Sonny's long-time friend and confidant who wants his pal to quit the business while he's still alive. Even Adam West from TV's Batman turns up playing himself (he's the leading actor in *The Spy Who Laughed at Danger*), though he doesn't get many scenes and makes less of a mark than the other familiar faces.

As you'd expect from a film about stuntmen, there are plenty of eye-popping stunts. A highlight is a 230-foot freefall from a helicopter performed by A.J. Bakunas. At the time, it was the highest freefall ever completed, though later that year the legendary Dar Robinson surpassed it. Tragically, Bakunas was killed trying to reclaim his record in September, 1978. He'd safely performed a fall from the ninth storey of a building for a scene in Steve Carver's *Steel*. He convinced Carver to let him re-do the fall from the 22nd storey, arguing that it would make a better spectacle in the finished film and would also give him a shot at claiming back his record. Alas, the airbag split on impact and Bakunas was severely injured, dying in hospital the following day. There's also a pretty impressive chariot sequence and a bruising barroom brawl which manages to be funny and raucous at the same time. It's all just a prelude to the big climax - an excellent sequence where towering chimneystacks topple and cars whiz beneath with milliseconds to spare and, of course, that exhilarating climactic gorge jump. The sequence was shot in Tuscaloosa, Alabama - the 'destroyed' bridge was a real one, located on Highway 78E, which was in the process of being demolished and rebuilt after sustaining structural damage in a traffic accident.

Hooper isn't high art, nor does it pretend to be. It might even seem shallow at first glance, though there is plenty going on for those willing to scratch the surface. Mostly though, it's lively and energetic and thrilling, with lots of good-natured charm and comic touches. The happiness and enthusiasm on set are infectious and result in a movie which is effortlessly entertaining. My main criticism would be that it is very smug, often pleased with itself and self-congratulatory. But that's only a very minor qualm - overall this is hugely enjoyable stuff, a worthy ode to those oh-so crazy stunt performers who do the unimaginable (and make it look easy) so that we can sit in our chairs and be thrilled by what we see. To those foolhardy men and women - we salute you!

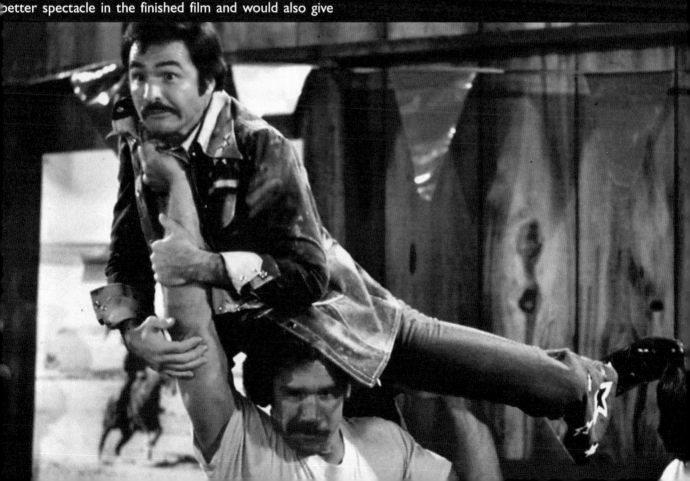

BUG

A Retrospective by David Flack

I discovered *Bug* (1975) on BBC2 (UK) during the famous horror double bills the channel used to screen late on Saturday nights. Like thousands of other viewers. I got a lot of pleasure and excitement from this series - especially the chance to see Universal, Hammer, AIP (and other) horror/sci-fi films from the '60s and '70s for the first time.

Bug was shown on 1st August, 1981, and was the second film on a double bill with *Bedlam* (1946). Both impressed me, but it was the 1975 entry that really startled me, being very different from other 'insects-on-the-rampage' films I'd seen. Until then, I'd only watched ones which featured giant-sized insects, such as the excellent *Them!* (1954) which boasted gigantic ants. The only film I'd seen which had normal sized insects on the rampage was *The Naked Jungle* (1954), in which soldier ants menace Charlton Heston and Eleanor Parker. The fire 'roaches in *Bug* were a little larger than normal, but wow were they different! It's fair to say the bugs and the film in general made quite an impression on me.

For this review, I rewatched *Bug* and was struck by how much it differs from the usual 'Creature Feature' formula. The copy I saw was rated PG, and this surprised me because it contains a number of nasty scenes and was certified 'X' when released. I would have expected it to still carry a UK 15 rating (or 'R' in America) at the very least. The film has its flaws, especially in the second half where, like its main character, it loses control. But overall, it is an intriguing, engrossing and quite disturbing picture.

The story is set in a small Californian town where the residents are suffering through a hot, steamy spell of weather. A scientist and part-time biology teacher, James Parmiter (Bradford Dillman), drops his wife Carrie (Joanna Miles) at church one Sunday morning. During the service, there is an earthquake. Luckily it doesn't cause much harm to the churchgoers, but it does damage the building. Among the congregation is Mr Tacker (Frederic Downs), a farmer, who is shocked and a little battered by the tremors. His son (Jesse Vint) arrives in a jeep to take him home. When they get back, they are met by Tacker's daughter and husband who are relieved to see them unharmed. Then the jeep suddenly bursts into flames, killing Tacker and his son. This is the first of many shock moments. The camera shows the jeep's exhaust pipe smoking while a cockroach scampers out.

The scene changes to a neighbouring farm where a young man, Gerald Metbaum (Richard Gilliland), is surveying the damage to his property. Hearing a loud clicking sound, he comes across a number of cockroaches coming out of a fissure caused by the earthquake. He picks one up and is surprised when he is burnt by the creature. There is a stray cat walking around, seemingly eating the 'roaches. Moments later, Gerald hears an unearthly wail and sees the unfortunate feline being attacked, its fur smoking as the 'roaches cover it and set it alight. It's a disturbing scene, and the cat really does look like it's in some distress.

We need a break after such a harrowing moment, and thankfully the action shifts to show Parmiter teaching biology at school. There's a charming sequence where a squirrel comes through the classroom window and Parmiter gently coaxes it to him to demonstrate the beauty of the bond between man and nature. Be warned, though - this is as light and gentle as this film gets! Watching the lesson is Gerald, who we learn is one of Parmiter's former pupils. He is carrying a box. They go to the school restaurant and Gerald asks Parmiter if he knows of any insects that can create fire. After being told no, he opens the box right in the middle of the restaurant and reveals the gruesome sight of the dead cat and bugs!

Gerald takes Parmiter to the farm and the scientist gets to see for himself what Gerald is talking about. Parmiter is burnt when he picks up one of the bugs. He is amazed to discover the creatures don't run away from people. He also discovers they have no eyes and the reason they set things alight is because they like to eat ash. They only have six legs and produce fire by rubbing them together. It seems the earthquake released them from their underground trappings.

Parmiter gradually becomes obsessed with the creatures, especially when he discovers them at home in his car exhaust and realises how they have been travelling around.

So far, the film has created a strong sense of foreboding and the ominous electronic soundtrack adds to the effect. The area is devastated by fires both domestic and in the brush and forests. Parmiter brings in his scientist friend Mark Ross (Alan Fudge) and they find the bugs' shells are like steel and are immune to poisons.

The fascination and obsession to learn more about these creatures makes Parmiter increasingly erratic and unstable. The film keeps throwing nastiness and shock scenes our way.

I won't spoil things by revealing too many of these shock moments, but one involving a bug in a telephone is very tense! Every time a phone rings from that moment on, you expect something awful to happen again! Parmiter's condition worsens when he experiences a personal tragedy caused by the bugs in another shocking and disturbing scene.

Admittedly, the second half loses something and gets a little too overwrought. Parmiter finds a way of killing some of the bugs, but he carries out insane experiments on others which make them even more dangerous. The exact nature of the experiments is rather vague, but apparently it's fully explained in 'The Hephaestus Plague' (the novel by Thomas Page upon which the film is based). There is another big twist

which reveals the bugs aren't mindless creatures - they have a disturbing level of intelligence which is increasing rapidly. They seem to use Parmiter as their vessel to gain control.

It all builds to a muddled, rather puzzling climax. Despite its unsatisfying ending, the film remains worth seeing - it is engrossing and gripping for most of the duration, and it helps that the bugs are a scary and original creation.

The film marked the last producing credit for the legendary William Castle. A producer, director, screenwriter and occasional actor, Castle's name usually makes movie fans think of the fun gimmicks he dreamed up to get bums on cinema seats. *Macabre* (1958), for example, with its life insurance for anyone that dies of fright; *The Tingler* (1959) with its electric shock cinema seats; *The House on Haunted Hill* (1959) with its plastic skeletons on a wire; or *13 Ghosts* (1960) with its 'ghost-viewer glasses'. He was behind other classic horrors too, including *Homicidal* (1961) and *Mr. Sardonicus* (1961). By the mid '60s, he was running out of ideas, but he hit it big when he bought the rights to Ira Levin's witchcraft novel 'Rosemary's Baby' with the intention of directing it. He ended up producing the film, while directing duties went to Polish filmmaker Roman Polanski. Released in 1968, it was a huge hit. Castle directed a few more films, the last being *Shanks* in 1974 (which he also produced). He died in 1977, aged 63.

Castle produced *Bug*, with direction being entrusted to French-born Jeannot Szwarc, making his cinematic debut after toiling in TV. Szwarc went on to direct other films in the genre, including *Jaws 2* (1978) and *Somewhere in Time* (1980).

The main role of James Parmiter is played by veteran character actor Bradford Dillman who had been in films and TV since the mid '50s. A solid and dependable actor, he certainly gives his all in *Bug*, going through various emotions. At the start, he's a knowledgeable, confident man; as things progress, he becomes frenzied as he is driven insane by the fantastic, horrific events engulfing him. No stranger to horror/sci-fi, he went on to appear in *Piranha* and *The Swarm* (both 1978) amongst many others. His career covered over 140 film and TV roles, and he died in 2018 at the age of 87.

All in all, this is a rather good, creepy - though ultimately uneven - addition to the creature feature genre. As mentioned, the fire 'roaches are genuinely scary and original, with competent special effects bringing them to life. On checking the closing credits, I noticed an animal trainer was credited but, rather worryingly, I couldn't see the statement "No animals were harmed in the making of this film", which makes me fearful about the scene with the unfortunate cat! I'm sure (at least, I hope!) it was all done with care, but it's quite harrowing and the noises from the poor feline are pretty disturbing. In fact, a lot of the death scenes are quite distressing… but isn't that the point? It proves the film's effectiveness - any good horror film should aim to distress its audience, and in that respect this one definitely does its job.

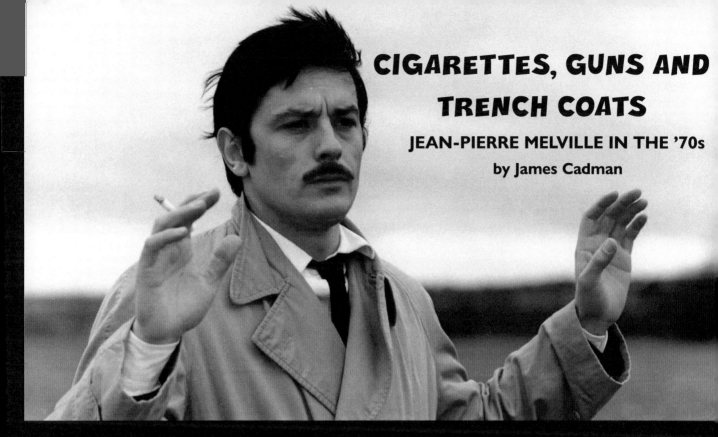

CIGARETTES, GUNS AND TRENCH COATS

JEAN-PIERRE MELVILLE IN THE '70s

by James Cadman

Writer-director Philippe Labro once said of his friend and mentor Jean-Pierre Melville: "Today, we say 'Melvillian' in the same way we say 'Fellinian' or 'Hitchcockian.' When an auteur becomes an adjective, you know they've reached their zenith." Labro was with Melville in Paris on an August evening in 1973 when the legendary filmmaker died suddenly at just 55 years of age.

Since he was a young child, Melville knew he wanted to make movies. When he was six years old, his parents bought him a 9.5mm Pathé Baby camera and, by the age of 22, he had shot the equivalent of 30 features in non-theatrical formats. His love of cinema grew rapidly with the advent of 'talkies' at the end of the '20s. He would sit for hours engrossed in the silent works of Buster Keaton, for example. Perhaps that explains the economy of words that would later characterise his own films: ambiguous moments of silence punctuated by short, sharp lines of dialogue and minimalist gestures.

A decade before Jean Seberg strolled down the Champs-Elysées in François Truffaut's *À bout de souffle*, Melville had already encountered many aspects that inspired him and would later fuel the young filmmakers of the *nouvelle vague*: the modern American literature synonymous with the 'Left Bank', the avant-garde works of Jean Cocteau and the jazz culture of post-war Paris. His inventiveness, the use of authentic locations, a reliance on a lean crew and the wonderfully innovative photography of Henri Decaë, all contributed to Melville being dubbed the 'godfather' of the New Wave. Along with Alexandre

Astruc, Alain Robbe-Grillet and Louis Malle, he belonged in an influential group known as 'La Transition.'

Melville was a maverick. Ruthlessly independent, he was one of few directors to fund and operate his own production studio, built on the site of a disused factory in a south-eastern *quartier* of Paris. He lived and worked there between 1953 and 1967, when much of the site was destroyed by fire. During those years, he hardly set foot outside and would often get up in the middle of the night to write and edit, when he knew he would be free of distraction. In fact, Melville was happiest when he was writing and editing; he actually found the process of filming a "tedious formality." During several fascinating interviews with Rui Nogueira he described himself as a 'craftsman'. To him, having his own studio, which included a cutting room and projector suite, was like having a 'cobbler's workshop.' In his words: "a director must be capable of doing everything."

Melville was passionate about American cinema, especially the '30s and '40s work of Fritz Lang, Frank Lloyd and William Wyler. At a time in the '50s when *film noir* was winding down in the US, he kept the genre alive into the '60s with two popular black and white crime thrillers, *Le Doulos* and *Le Deuxième souffle*. He breathed new life into a world in which laconic men in trench coats entered the room with a gun in each hand. It is almost impossible to watch any of his films from the turn of the '60s without seeing echoes of *The Big Heat* and *Dead End*.

In the quarter century between 1947 and 1972, made

films. They are highly personal, understated and possess a sense of cool that was way ahead of its time. His characters mainly inhabit a romanticised world of heroes and villains, living and dying by a certain code of honour, where mood and style come before plot.

Interestingly, in a 1970 interview Melville said he felt uncertain how his films would be received in the future, wondering if they "will have aged terribly." He also predicted that the "final disappearance of cinemas will take place around the year 2020" and that "there will be nothing but television." With their contemporary, stylised feel, even his harshest critics could not deny that his films have aged exceptionally well. Indeed, many modern-day filmmakers, including John Woo and Quentin Tarantino, have paid tribute to his influence.

Let's explore the only two films he made in the '70s, beginning with *Le Cercle rouge*.

Le Cercle rouge (1970)

Although *Le Samouraï* is widely considered his masterpiece, *Le Cercle rouge* is quintessential Melville. By some margin, it is also his most commercially successful picture, selling more than 4.3 million tickets in France alone.

Le Cercle rouge centres on a three-way partnership: two professional crooks, ex-con Corey (the steely, blue-eyed Alain Delon), just released from prison, and Vogel (the less memorable Gian Maria Volonté), who is on the run having escaped from a train bound for Paris. With Vogel hiding in Corey's boot, the pair head to Paris by car. It is here that they meet with the third man, an alcoholic ex-cop, Jansen (expertly played by Yves Montand), who happens to be a skilled marksman.

Before he was released from prison, Corey received a tip-off from a corrupt guard of the perfect 'job', an exclusive jewellery store in Paris. It is at this point that the three men are drawn more tightly into the 'red circle' of their common destiny. The bonds that knit Corey, Vogel and Jansen together ultimately seal their fate.

This would not be a classic French *policier* without the full force of the law hot on their trail. Having failed to track down Vogel as he fled into the countryside, Inspector Matteï (Bourvil) is instructed to use all means at his disposal to find the men. Like his quarry, the determined inspector is a loner. We immediately warm to him as we see him return to his apartment and observe his domestic routine of running the bath and attending to his cats. As Matteï, Bourvil is an inspired choice, one of the film's many highlights.

At one point we see Matteï called into a meeting with Marchand, the Director of Internal Affairs at Quai des Orfèvres. In a prophetic exchange of dialogue, Marchand tells Matteï that innocence does not exist, that crime lives in every man and it is just a matter of flushing it out.

"Men are all guilty ... they come into the world innocent but it does not last." It is as if Melville, who also wrote the screenplay, constructed his film on this statement - an effort to mythologise the criminal condition. He did at one point describe *Le Cercle rouge* as a "transposed western, with the action taking place in Paris instead of the West... with cars instead of horses."

In a film where women barely feature, all we can do is ponder over the connections between the male characters and the rules of right and wrong that the gangsters live by. Melville saw the gangster story as the ideal vehicle for the 'modern tragedy.' Since the American *film noir* flicks of the '30s and '40s, it has proved a versatile genre where it is possible to portray the full spectrum of betrayal, friendship, honour and loyalty.

By far the most exciting set piece of the entire film is the meticulously planned and executed robbery of the jewellery store in Paris' Place Vendôme. The robbery itself lasts nearly half an hour; during that time there is no dialogue and only subtle music, yet it makes for truly riveting cinema, an exercise in timing and tension. The suspense grabs us from the moment Corey and Vogel arrive on the scene. From rooftop silhouettes against a rich, blue Paris skyline, Henri Decaë's camera tracks their every move as they cross empty courtyards and enter dark stairwells. Their journey to the gems is just as captivating as the robbery itself, especially when sharpshooter Jansen arrives to help them bypass the security system. In true Melville style, with its hi-tech surveillance cameras and laser-beams, there is a wonderfully modern vibe to this entire sequence.

Since being captivated by John Huston's *The Asphalt Jungle*, Melville had wanted to make a heist film. He has brilliantly assembled all the winning components of his earlier crime yarns and woven them together to create a humdinger of a caper. In his own words, Melville has created "a digest of all my thrillers." Although long, at 140 minutes, *Le Cercle rouge* never lets up. Each scene is carefully constructed with new details emerging at every viewing.

Un flic (1972)

At the time of its release in October 1972, Melville's final film, *Un flic*, did not receive a warm reception from French critics. Negative words such as 'boring', 'embarrassing' and 'incoherent' were peppered throughout the popular press. I will confess, when I first saw the film a few years ago (it was the first Melville film I had seen), I found it dull and forgettable. There were uncomfortable plot holes, long moments of silence and reflection and an oddly underused Catherine Deneuve; Melville loved to augment his films with major stars and Deneuve was among the leading female players of the '70s.

Revisiting the film to write this article, I saw qualities

Un flic that I had failed to appreciate before. The only explanation I can offer is that I had since become more familiar with Melville's work and grown more receptive to his abstract, layered style. 'Layered' is a good word since, in a 1962 interview with *Télérama*, Melville said he would like his films to be "like a *millefeuilles* cake: two very different, pleasing substances, pastry and cream." He wanted the "real gourmets" to taste the pastry while those with "less fine taste" would only taste the cream. Ten years later, his ambition for *Un flic* was surely the same - to create a crime thriller that, on one level, would be an entertaining piece of cinema, while on the other, would offer a deeper, more philosophical experience.

The 'cop' referred to in the film's title is Paris Inspector Coleman, played by an ashen-faced Alain Delon. A rather wooden but physically imposing Richard Crenna plays Coleman's friend and nightclub owner, Simon, who happens to lead the very gang of bank robbers and drug runners Coleman is pursuing. Their lives are intertwined by the fact that both men are in love with Cathy, the smouldering yet practically mute Deneuve.

Like many of Melville's films, *Un flic* opens with a quote designed to set the scene for the events to follow. The quote, from François-Eugène Vidocq, an escaped convict who became Chief of Police, translates to: "The only feelings man could ever inspire in the policeman are ambiguity and derision." As Melville scholar Ginette Vincendeau noted: '*Un flic* will be a meditation on ambiguity (legal, moral or sexual) and derision." It is a clear nod to Melville's fascination for the thin line between the law and crime - the good and the bad, heroes and villains. When Melville approached Delon, he offered him a choice between the role of Simon and that of Coleman. The fact that he chose the latter was inspired; in his previous Melville films he had played the villain and now the audience had to accept he was on the side of the law. Only his badge distinguishes him from the cool crooks of *Le Samouraï* and *Le Cercle rouge*.

It is impossible to review *Un flic* without referring to the two memorable set pieces that take up a large portion of the action. Both are dazzling heist sequences. The first of these occupies the opening 15 minutes as Simon and his gang are seen cruising along a deserted road in a seaside resort town on the west coast of France. They are on their way to rob a bank and Melville delights in taking us through every step of their operation. He hikes up the tension as the men enter the bank, one by one, fighting their way through driving rain lashing in from the sea. Just as he had achieved with *Le Cercle rouge*, the sequence is as visually striking as it is thrilling; in his first and only collaboration with Melville, photographer Walter Wottitz creates a dream-like atmosphere filled with stony greys, blues and greens.

A similar effect is achieved later in the film in the second robbery where we see Simon skilfully lowered by helicopter onto a moving train. He is on a daring mission to lift a haul of drugs bound for Lisbon before it is intercepted by the border police. The scene is notable for how Melville handles the notion of time lapse. We see one of Simon's gang glance at his watch and announce: "He's got ten minutes left." And Melville edits precisely ten minutes of energetic, claustrophobic footage, culminating in Crenna being winched back up to the helicopter, complete with suitcases of heroin. Many critics complained that the excitement and spectacle was hampered by the obvious use of models to create the desired effect. Whilst this may be so, it could be argued that Melville did this deliberately. Years before *Un flic*, he told an interviewer: "I'd like my films to stop resembling reality and, more and more, to become dream-like adventures." Even before the train sequence, Wottitz's camera had paraded past a long line of ultramodern apartment buildings as he tracked the villains on their way to the bank. Later we witnessed Coleman, a French police inspector with an American-sounding name, driving around in a huge American car, entering a futuristic Paris office block.

Melville once said that, long after his death, *Un flic* would be considered his masterpiece. If this is not the case, it cannot be argued that Melville's last film is among his most daring, a film whose astonishing beauty grows with each viewing. It is interesting to consider if its many experimental features award us a glimpse into the style Melville may have adopted had he gone on to make more films during the '70s. Nearly 50 years after its release there has never been a better time to revisit it and to wonder.

CLOSING CREDITS

Simon J. Ballard

Simon lives in Oxford and works in its oldest building, a Saxon Tower. Whilst also working in the adjoining church, he has never felt tempted to re-enact scenes from *Taste the Blood of Dracula* or *Dracula A.D.1972*. He has never done this. Ever. He regularly contributes to the magazine 'We Belong Dead' and its various publications, and once read Edgar Allan Poe's 'The Black Cat' to a garden full of drunk young people at his local gay pub The Jolly Farmers. His first published work was a Top Tip in 'Viz' of which he is justifiably proud.

Rachel Bellwoar

Rachel is a writer for 'Comicon', 'Diabolique' magazine and 'Flickering Myth'. If she could have any director fim a biopic about her life it would be Aki Kaurismäki.

David Michael Brown

David is a British ex-pat living in Sydney. Working as a freelance writer he has contributed to 'The Big Issue', 'TV Week', 'GQ', 'Rolling Stone' and 'Empire Magazine Australia', where he was Senior Editor for almost eight years. He is presently writing a book on the film music of German electronic music pioneers Tangerine Dream and researching the work of Andy Warhol associate and indie filmmaker Paul Morrissey for a forthcoming project.

James Cadman

James first discovered his love of films as a child in the 1980s, happily scanning the shelves of his local video shop. Into his 20s, as part of his media degree, he secured work experience with a major film company which included visiting the set of *Notting Hill* at Shepperton Studios. Now living in Derbyshire with his wife and two young children, James enjoys watching and researching films, especially the '70s work of Eastwood, Friedkin, Peckinpah and Scorsese.

Dawn Dabell

Dawn runs her own clothing business in West Yorkshire. When she's not busy selling fabulous dresses and quirky tops, she's a full-time film enthusiast, writer and mum! She has written for 'Cinema Retro', 'We Belong Dead', 'Monster!' and 'Weng's Chop', and is also the co-author of 'More Than a Psycho: The Complete Films of Anthony Perkins' (2018) and 'Ultimate Warrior: The Complete Films of Yul Brynner' (2019). She is also the co-creator and designer of the very mag you're holding in your hands right now.

Jonathon Dabell

Jonathon was born in Nottingham in 1976. He is a huge film fan and considers '70s cinema his favourite decade. He has written for 'Cinema Retro' and 'We Belong Dead', and co-authored 'More Than a Psycho: The Complete Films of Anthony Perkins' and 'Ultimate Warrior: The Complete Films of Yul Brynner' with his wife. He lives in Yorkshire with his wife, three kids, three cats and two rabbits!

David Flack

David was born and bred in Cambridge. Relatively new to the writing game, he has had reviews published in 'We Belong Dead' and 'Cinema of the '70s'. He loves watching, talking, reading and writing about film and participating on film forums. The best film he has seen in over 55 years of watching is *Jaws* (1975). The worst is *The Creeping Terror* (1963) or anything by Andy Milligan.

John H. Foote

John is a critic/film historian with thirty years experience. He has been a film critic on TV, radio, print criticism, newspaper and the web, for various sites including his own, Footeandfriendsonfilm.com. He spent ten years as Director of the Toronto Film School, where he taught Film History, and has written two books. The first was an exploration of the films directed by Clint Eastwood, the second a massive volume of the works of Steven Spielberg. Scorsese is next. John has interviewed everyone in film, except Jack Nicholson he quips. His obsession with film began at age 13.

John Harrison

John is a Melbourne, Australia-based freelance writer and film historian who has written for numerous genre publications, including 'Fatal Visions', 'Cult Movies', 'Is It Uncut?', 'Monster!' and 'Weng's Chop'. Harrison is also the author of the Headpress book 'Hip Pocket Sleaze: The Lurid World of Vintage Adult Paperbacks', has recorded audio commentaries for Kino Lorber, and composed the booklet essays for the Australian Blu-ray releases of *Thirst*, *Dead Kids* and *The Survivor*. 'Wildcat!', Harrison's book on the film and television career of former child evangelist Marjoe Gortner, was published by Bear Manor in 2020.

Julian Hobbs

Julian's lifelong love of scary movies began when he was 5 or 6, after being severely traumatized by a TV screening of George Pal's *War of the Worlds*. Several decades later later, Mark Berry asked him to contribute some DVD reviews to his 'Naked' magazine (no, not that kind of mag…) and the film writing bug caught him. He has written for 'We Belong Dead' and its various book offshoots. If he wasn't writing, he'd be beating the skins quite loudly in various Bristol bands. Julian is currently employed within the private health sector after a stint supporting the NHS.

Kev Hurst

Kev is a Nottingham FE college teacher of film and animation and a historian of all things cinematic. He is a massive physical film and TV collector who spends way too much time browsing the shelves of his local CEX store. He is an avid fan of all genres but has passionate interests in all things horror and sci-fi related, from body horror to giallo, dystopian fiction to steampunk. His favourite filmmakers are basically all 'The Movie Brats' and well-respected horror directors like John Carpenter, David Cronenberg, John Landis, Dario Argento, Mario Bava, Tobe Hooper and George A. Romero.

Darren Linder

Darren grew up in the '70s and has been forever enamored with films from that decade. He is a lifelong resident of Oregon, currently living in Portland. He has performed in many rock bands, ran a non-profit dog rescue, and worked in social service with at-risk youths. Currently he works security in music venues, and is completing a book about his experiences there to be published later this year. His favorite film directors of the '70s are Sam Peckinpah, Francis Ford Coppola and William Friedkin.

Brian J. Robb

Brian is the 'New York Times' and 'Sunday Times' bestselling biographer of Leonardo Di Caprio, Keanu Reeves, Johnny Depp and Brad Pitt. He has also written books on silent cinema, the films of Philip K. Dick, horror director Wes Craven, and classic comedy team Laurel and Hardy, the *Star Wars* movies, Superheroes, Gangsters, and Walt Disney, as well as science fiction television series *Doctor Who* and *Star Trek*. His illustrated books include a History of Steampunk and an award-winning guide to J.R.R. Tolkien's Middle-earth. A former magazine and newspaper editor, he was co-founder of the Sci-Fi bulletin website and lives near Edinburgh.

Allen Rubinstein

Allen grew up in an upper-middle-class neighborhood in suburban Connecticut. He writes about movies and history and tries to reveal the truth wherever possible. He works with his wife on a teaching organization called The Poetry Salon (www.thepoetrysalon.com) in Costa Rica while taking care of far too many cats. He has not yet told his parents that he's an anarcho-syndicalist.

Peter Sawford

Peter was born in Essex in 1964 so considers himself a child of the '70s. A self-confessed film buff, he loves watching, reading about and talking about cinema. A frustrated writer his whole life, he's only recently started submitting what he writes to magazines. His favourite director is Alfred Hitchcock with Billy Wilder running him a close second. He still lives in Essex with his wife and works as an IT trainer and when not watching films he's normally panicking over who West Ham are playing next.

Aaron Stielstra

Aaron was born in Ann Arbor, Michigan and grew up in Tucson, AZ. and NYC. He is an actor, writer, illustrator, soundtrack composer and director. After moving to Italy in 2012, he has appeared in 4 spaghetti westerns and numerous horror-thrillers - all of them unnecessarily wet. He recently directed the punk rock comedy *Excretion: the Shocking True Story of the Football Moms*. His favorite '70s actor is Joe Spinell.

Ian Taylor

Ian dabbled in horror fiction in the early '90s before writing and editing music fanzines. He later adjudicated plays for the Greater Manchester Drama Federation but enjoys film analysis most. Over the last five years, he has become a regular writer and editorial team member for 'We Belong Dead' magazine and contributed to all their book releases. This has led to writing for Dez Skinn's 'Halls of Horror', Allan Bryce's 'Dark Side' and Hemlock's 'Fantastic Fifties', amongst others. His first solo book 'All Sorts of Things Might Happen: The Films of Jenny Agutter' was recently released as a 'We Belong Dead' publication.

Dr Andrew C. Webber

Dr W has been a Film, Media and English teacher and examiner for over 35 years and his passion for the cinema remains undiminished all these years later. As far as he is concerned, a platform is where you wait for the 08.16 to Victoria; dropping is something that louts do with litter; and streaming is how you might feel if you were in *Night of the Hunter* being hotly pursued by Robert Mitchum with "Hate" tattooed on his knuckles and Stanley Cortez doing the cinematography.

Printed in Great Britain
by Amazon